THE TWO

M000014178

Tremble Before God Alone

Chris Poblete
Cruciform Press | Released April, 2012

To the beautiful Alyssa, a God-fearing woman
(a la Proverbs 31:30) who, next to Jesus,
is the clearest example of God's grace in my life.
May the Lord grant us many years of faithfulness
in marriage and ministry.
– Chris Poblete

CruciformPress

"I don't know about you, but most of the things I grapple with in ministry, and in my own life, are summed up in two issues: We are too scared; and we aren't scared enough. This book by Chris Poblete points the way to crucify our fear of man and to rightly order our fear of God. Reading this book will prompt you to seek in your own life the biblical tension between 'fear not' and 'fear God.'"

Russell D. Moore, Dean, The Southern Baptist Theological Seminary

"Our lives can be guided by what we fear, and Chris Poblete wants us to fear the Lord! He unpacks for us, through the lens of God's revealed character and the gospel, that fearing the Lord is not some cheap cliché, but a blood-bought gift for his people that leads to repentance, thankfulness, adoration and worship."

Darren Carlson, President and Founder, Training Leaders International

"A.W. Pink lamented that 'the God of the twentieth century … commands the respect of no really thoughtful man … The God of many a present-day pulpit is an object of pity rather than awe-inspiring fear.' What Pink said of the 20th century rings true today when downsized deities and consumer-friendly "Christs" are a dime a dozen. Chris Poblete has written an importantly countercultural book, moving us beyond a homeboy God we could fist-bump to a holy God we can worship. *The Two Fears* helps us recover a biblical fear of God and all the awe, repentance, and freedom from self-centered fears that go with it. An awesome resource!"

Dr. Thaddeus Williams, Biola University; author, *Love, Freedom, and Evil: Does Authentic Love Require Free Will?*

"Chris Poblete is an artist and his book, *The Two Fears*, will take you on an engaging, picturesque journey through the orchard of fearing God. Along this path of wisdom, he will linger long enough for you to pluck its fruit and savor the richness of its gospel flavor, leading you to worship God as you forsake the lesser enticements of this world. By God's grace, you will be freed from unholy fear and its fruits, and instead, enabled to embrace a lifestyle of faith and a habit of God-fearing worship: generosity instead of self-entitlement, humility instead of arrogance, reverence rather than indifference, dependence rather than doubt, obedience instead of revolt, and faith instead of faithlessness. The clarity and sobriety of *The Two Fears* will show you how to enjoy God as you magnify Christ and walk by the power of his Spirit. I commend this book to you: it will fuel your worship and empower your discipleship."

Gabe Tribbett, Director of Life Education and Leadership Development, Christ's Covenant Church, Winona Lake, IA

"Those who find themselves struggling relate to God and man in a way that is balanced and biblical will find an excellent guide in *The Two Fears* by Chris Poblete. This simple and direct book confronts and redirects our misplaced fear of man, reminding us of truths that instill a fear of God that is both biblical and life-affirming."

Richard H. Clark, co-founder, Editor-in-chief, *Christ and Pop Culture*

"Readers will be equally challenged and blessed as they read *The Two Fears* and heed Chris Poblete's call to embrace a holy fear of God—one that doesn't cause us to cower in terror, but empowers us to move forward in Christ's mission, entranced by the beauty and wonder of the cross of Christ."

Aaron Armstrong, author, *Awaiting a Savior* and *Contend*

"The writer of Hebrews teaches us that 'It is a fearful thing to fall into the hands of the living God' (Hebrews 10:31). The writer of Proverbs states that the fear of the Lord is the beginning of wisdom and knowledge (Proverbs 1:7; 9:10). Poblete not only stirs us up to this truth, but teaches us what it means to fear God, that we stand in awe of God by hearing and heeding his Word in Scripture, and that the fear of the Lord will set us free. One who learns to fear the Lord need fear nothing else, for though God's wrath is fearful, his mercy is awing as well. I hope you will hear Chris out, and that his book will teach us to both tremble and rejoice in the majesty of our God."

Brad Williams, pastor, New Covenant Baptist Church, contributor, *Christ and Pop Culture*

"In this excellent and easy to read book, Chris Poblete tackles a topic that is often overlooked in contemporary Christian theology. As he examines an unhealthy fear of man and the fear of God, he leads his readers straight into the throne room of the One who is sovereign in and over all things — the One who is wisdom from God — the Lord Jesus Christ. Read this book, but beware — rather than you examining it, the Word of God will examine you and encourage you to consider that the God of the Bible is far more majestic and glorious than you ever dared to imagine."

Dave Jenkins, Director, Servants of Grace Ministries

"This timely book enters into a church context where 'God-fearing' is out of vogue. Combining biblical passages, theological categories, pastoral wisdom, and his personal story, Poblete has given us a needed reminder of how important it is to be God-fearers if we seek to know God and live for him."

Jared Oliphint Regional Coordinator, Westminster Theological Seminary; Contributor, Reformed Forum

"In this practical and very readable book, Chris Poblete describes a side of our culture — the absence of fear. 'Where have the God-fearers gone?' he asks. He shows how both the absence of true fear and the presence of 'unholy [false] fear' stem from an absence of a knowledge of the awesome God of the Bible, and that, in meeting him, we discover the real dimensions of creational existence and the wonderful benefits of living in fear and deep respect before him, freed from the '[false] fear of men.'"

Peter Jones, PhD, Executive Director, TruthXchange; Scholar-in-Residence and Adjunct Professor, Westminster Seminary in California

Table of Contents

CruciformPress
something new in Christian publishing

Our Books: Short. Clear. Concise. Helpful. Inspiring. Gospel-focused. *Print; ebook formats: Mobi, ePub, PDF.*

Monthly Releases: A new book each month.

Consistent Prices: Every book costs the same.

Subscription Options: Print books or ebooks delivered to you every month, at a discount. Or buy print books or ebooks individually.

Prepaid or Monthly Subscriptions
Print Book . . . . $6.49 per month
Ebook   . . . . $3.99 per month

Non-Subscription Sales
1-5 Print Books . . . . $8.45 each
6-50 Print Books . . . . $7.45 each
More than 50 Print Books . . . . $6.45 each
Single Ebooks (bit.ly/CPebks) . . . . $5.45 each

---

The Two Fears - Tremble Before God Alone

Print ISBN: 978-1-936760-50-3
ePub ISBN: 978-1-936760-52-7
Mobipocket ISBN: 978-1-936760-51-0

INTRODUCTION

Most Christians will agree that we ought to love our God. But what about fearing God? The Bible says that "the fear of the LORD is the beginning of wisdom" (Proverbs 9:10), yet an honest assessment of modern evangelicalism would suggest that we do not today give the fear of God nearly that level of respect. Many Christians seem to assume that the gospel of grace trumps the fear of the Lord, and that wisdom now has some source other than godly fear. Yet only the God of the gospel is truly worthy of our reverential fear.

Encouraging a group of Christians, the apostle Peter wrote: "conduct yourselves with fear throughout the time of your exile" (1 Peter 1:17). Life is an "exile," a short passing through on the way to our true home. And apparently we are to live this exile in godly fear. But what does that mean? And what does that *not* mean? What is good fear and what is bad fear? The Bible offers us a standard for the pursuit of answers, an explicitly active standard:

My son, if you *receive* my words
    and *treasure up* my commandments with you,
making your ear attentive to wisdom

and *inclining* your heart to understanding;
yes, if you *call out* for insight
 and *raise your voice* for understanding,
if you *seek it* like silver
 and *search for it* as for hidden treasures,
then you will understand the fear of the LORD
 and find the knowledge of God.
For the LORD gives wisdom;
 from his mouth come knowledge and
understanding. (Proverbs 2:1-6)

My hope is that in the coming pages you will embrace every active verb in this passage from Proverbs—that you will receive, treasure, listen to, incline your heart, call out for insight, raise your voice, seek and search with all your might for holy reverence and the fear of the LORD.

As you do, the promise could not be more clear: then you will understand. Then you will fear. Then you will find.

One

THE NATURE OF FEAR

Along the Southern Californian coast is a short strip of sand called Aliso Creek Beach. Lined with picnic tables and fire pits, it's a popular place for afternoon picnics, family outings, and beach bonfires.

The college group I attended early in my Christian life frequented this spot every summer. I'll never forget one of these afternoon gatherings. A thick blanket of clouds hid the California sun, unusual for a summer in Orange County. The ocean breeze was especially chilly and the water was much too cold for good sense. Despite the conditions, my friend Chase and I decided to jump into the freezing ocean to see who could withstand it the longest. I cannot for the life of me remember what prompted such an idiotic dare, but it probably had something to do with the fact that sixty of our peers were shouting, "You guys are crazy!" I'm sure my 20-year-old self had something to prove that day, although I can't recall what.

The water was ice cold. The kind of cold that makes your diaphragm go rubbery once your chest hits the water and you feel stupid because you suddenly forget how to breathe properly. In our contest of resolve, however, I had a secret. What Chase didn't know is that I used to play this game by myself when I was a small kid. I would jump into the family pool in the winter and, with chattering teeth and shaky breaths, I would grin and bear it until I could breathe normally again. In this water-treading face-off with Chase, I felt like a natural. After about a minute in the ocean, just as my lungs had reclaimed the ability to take full breaths, Chase began his shivering retreat to shore.

Instead of swimming in to claim my victory, I made a decision that would almost claim my life. A new believer at the time, I wanted all my new Christian friends to notice how crazy cool I was. As my pride swelled to biblical proportions, I swam out further from shore, just past the point where the waves break, and began floating on my back. I lay there in the frigid water—a demonstration of foolish arrogance if there ever was one—warmed by the thought that everyone onshore must be marveling at my stamina. When I switched back to treading water and my ears resurfaced, I immediately knew I had a bigger problem than just being cold. Instead of the noise of 60 college students on a beach all I could hear was waves. I scanned the shore for their bonfire and finally found it about 200 yards north. I had been drifting in a rip current.

The current was aggressively pulling me both further south and farther out from shore. I started swimming toward the beach, but every yard I went forward, I drifted at least another yard back. Soon I was almost half a mile south of the bonfire, and no closer to shore. Waves started to break over my head and my muscles began to cramp. For the first time in my life, I feared the ocean. I suddenly realized that behind me lay an infinite amount of water, and below me in the depths lurked … I had no idea.

I gasped for air but swallowed seawater instead. Just as I began to admit to myself that I couldn't last much longer, a wave drove me under and tumbled my body like clothes in a washing machine. I tried to swim back up, but I had no idea which way up was. I almost stopped fighting, but instead for some reason I cried out silently to God for help. And at that very instant a wave pushed my head above water, I took a full breath of air, and my limp body rode the lip of that wave all the way to the beach like a dumb plank of wood that had learned how to surf.

Lying there in the sand gasping, all I could say was, "Thank you, Jesus. Thank you, Jesus."

That afternoon, I discovered both humiliation and a fear of the ocean I had never known before. In God's good providence, this experience also gave me my definition of fear:

To fear something is to give credence to its power over you.

Credence is not a word we hear a lot. Let me explain.

When children are afraid of the dark, they give credence to the power that darkness has over them—fear of what could be lurking in the shadows. When one fears being alone, he gives credence to the power of loneliness over him—he accepts as true the possibility that he will never experience fulfilling companionship. Think of other things that people are commonly afraid of: drowning, heights, spiders, snakes, clowns, conflict, public speaking, suffering ... the list goes on. But God is rarely on that list. Why is that? How does God, the creator who transcends space and time, not make the cut? Should he?

Again, when we fear something, we give credence to its power over us. If you fear the ocean, your heart will pound when currents pull you away from land. If you fear heights, your knees will wobble when you approach the edge of a 12-story balcony.

And if you fear God, your heart will quake at the smallest glimpse of his majesty.

Consider the prophet Isaiah when he became undone before God enthroned: "Woe is me!," he confessed, "For I am lost; for I am a man of unclean lips, and I dwell in the midst of a people of unclean lips; for my eyes have seen the King, the LORD of hosts!" (6:5). For Isaiah, to see God's glory and majesty was to immediately acknowledge God's power over him. The fragility of his own sinfulness came instantly clear as he stood before God's holiness.

A Fear Forbidden, a Fear Commanded

Some say we don't need to fear God anymore. They say this grand picture of God in Isaiah is the Old Testament God—or God of the Law—and that the New Testament God is best represented as Jesus, "Meek and Mild"—a Jesus that we shouldn't fear, a God of grace. After all, they argue, "There is no fear in love, but perfect love casts out fear" (1 John 4:18). Yet when the man who penned those words—John, the beloved disciple of Jesus—saw a vision of the risen Christ at Patmos, he fell at his feet as though dead (Revelation 1:17).

The fear of the Lord is commended throughout Scripture. Let's look at just a few examples:

- God rewarded Abraham for his fear: "Do not lay your hand on the boy or do anything to him, for now I know that you fear God, seeing you have not withheld your son, your only son, from me" (Genesis 22:12).
- Fearing God is akin to loving your neighbor: "You shall not wrong one another, but you shall fear your God, for I am the Lord your God" (Leviticus 25:17).
- Fear is a way to serve the Lord: "Serve the Lord with fear, and rejoice with trembling" (Psalm 2:11).
- Fear is pure: "The fear of the Lord is pure, enduring forever" (Psalm 19:9, HCSB).
- Fear is a mark of faithfulness: "By faith Noah, being warned by God concerning events as yet unseen, in reverent fear constructed an ark for the saving of his household" (Hebrews 11:7).
- Fear is something we will still know in heaven: "And from the throne came a voice, saying, 'Praise our God, all you his servants, you who fear him, small and great!'" (Revelation 19:5).

At the same time, Scripture also warns against fear. When the Israelites gathered at the foot of Mount Sinai, they saw thunder and flashes of lightning and heard trumpets blaring before a mountain billowing in smoke. As a result, they were utterly terrified. Moses then spoke puzzling words to them: "Do not fear, for God has come to test you, that the fear of him may be before you, that you may not sin" (Exodus 20:20). Here, Moses commands the nation of Israel both to fear God and not to fear God. So which is it? *To fear or not to fear?* How do we explain this seeming contradiction? John Bunyan clarifies, "that fear which already had taken possession of them, was not the fear of God, but a fear that was of Satan, of their own misjudging hearts, and so a fear that was ungodly." [1]

Bunyan goes on to say that there are two types of fear: "a fear forbidden, and a fear commended." [2] Other fellow Puritans and Reformers have echoed these sentiments, careful to affirm a biblical distinction between the two fears:

- For Stephen Charnock, it was the difference between bondage fear and reverential fear.
- For George Swinnock, it was the difference between filial fear and servile fear.
- For John Gill, it was the difference between idolatrous fear and worshipful fear.
- For Charles Spurgeon, it was fear that draws men further from God versus fear that drives men toward God.

Today, however, many evangelical churches—especially those in the West—treat the fear of the Lord as a taboo subject. There is no distinction between good fear and bad fear. To us, all fear is bad fear. Fear is so un-Western, so unsophisticated, so unfashionable.

Talk about the fear of the Lord with Christians in

some rural areas of Rwanda and Uganda, however, as I have, and you will see how quick they are to get this notion of godly fear. They understand that God is mighty and they are not. They understand that they are dependent upon God to send rain so that they can grow food, and eat, and drink, and live.

When a Ugandan Muslim girl asked us what the religious landscape looked like in America, we included atheism in our response. Confused, she asked, "What is atheism?" When she learned that atheism is the belief that there is no God, she was floored: "Not believe in a god?!"

Even though this young woman did not believe in the God of the Bible, she knew enough about our fallen world from living in an impoverished Ugandan village that she could easily acknowledge that she was not entitled to anything. She knew to be thankful for simple things like food and shelter. She knew she answered to something, or Someone, bigger than herself for her very existence.

In contrast, Christians in the West—myself included—often feel entitled to what we have. From the roof overhead to the car in the garage to the technology in our pockets to the relative freedom and stability of our society—we feel we simply deserve it all.

This attitude creeps into the church, threatening our humility and, consequently, our worship. But a godly fear of the Lord requires that we give credence to the God who has power over us:

- the power to give and to take away
- the power to form us in a mother's womb

- the power to know when we lie down and when we rise up
- the power to regenerate a heart of stone
- the power to number our days
- the power to enthrone rulers and make kingdoms fall
- the power to do whatever he pleases

Our God holds the power to save sinners, to reverse death, to destroy the bonds of Satan and sin. He is the mighty Savior and great Redeemer who can regenerate a heart, reform it from the inside out, and keep it for all eternity.

Do you know this God? Do you know the power he has over you? Do you acknowledge — give credence to — his power? His majesty? His splendor? His *being*?

This is godly fear. It is the fear of the Lord.

When we reject the notion that fear should characterize our approach to God, we rob ourselves of a worshipful delight that can only come through reverential fear. In his commentary on Psalm 22, John Calvin writes, "The fear which [David] recommends is not, however, such as would frighten the faithful from approaching God, but that which will bring them truly humbled into his sanctuary."[3]

For the Christian, the fear of the Lord does not diminish the gospel of grace; it amplifies it. This reverential fear makes his grace more amazing, his mercy more grand, his justice more right, and his love more astounding.

The deeper our understanding of what it means to fear a holy God, the better able we will be to fear him as he ought to be feared, and the better able we will be to worship him as he ought to be worshiped.

Two
A GOD WHO IS NOT LIKE US

I know a lot of creative types, from writers and musicians to painters and photographers. I've watched them engage in their craft and I know that each discipline requires two things: a tool in hand and a canvas of one sort or another to mark upon. This is how creativity works. An artist must start with something. She needs a pencil or an instrument or a brush, and she needs something to alter. She can't work with nothing.

God works with nothing. All he needs is the sheer volition of his will.

The first words spoken in the universe were, "Let there be light" (Geneses 1:3). Before they were uttered, there was nothing. No time. No matter. Only a dark void. And guess what happened after this command was delivered? Well, there was *light.*

Try to wrap your mind around that one. Something came out of nothing because Someone spoke it as so.

I can't make that happen. What about you? Walk down the timeline of Genesis 1, and you'll notice that

God is always the subject of the sentence while creation is always its predicate.

God is not like us. And we are not like him.

As elementary as this may seem, if we want to understand the fear of the Lord, we must begin with the knowledge that God is not like us. It's worth relearning and remembering. For the one who concedes this fact, the rewards are great.

Calvin said that true wisdom "consists almost entirely of two parts: the knowledge of God and of ourselves."[4] And he rightly observed that these two are interconnected. A right view of one will inform a right view of the other.

Such a high view of God is central to godly fear. Jeremiah asked, "Who would not fear you, O King of the nations?" He then answers his rhetorical question with a humble confession: "For this is your due; for among all the wise ones of the nations and in all their kingdoms there is none like you" (Jeremiah 10:7).

When we meditate upon the incomparable nature of God, our esteem for self and other idols fizzles away, extinguished under the weight of his majesty. But all too often, we grow numb and dull to this spiritual reality. Instead, we want Jesus the God-man to be our homeboy, a friend who is on our level—who wears our clothes and speaks our language and shares our idiosyncrasies. As someone once told me, we forfeit God's transcendence by overemphasizing his immanence—that he is present and his help available to us. This is a grave mistake.

Yes, God is immanent and deeply involved in the lives of his creatures. He certainly is not the apathetic God of deism who retreated eons ago to his ivory tower in the sky. He is a personally involved High Priest and dear friend to sinners. But the awe-inspiring wonder of God's immanence finds its full meaning not in an "I'm just like you, homeboy" persona, but rather in his holy and transcendent nature. Although he is the Lord God Almighty, he chose to leave his throne in heaven and condescend to save a fallen people. That's why we sing of his grace as *amazing*. He is more than a tender friend; he is a fearsomely merciful Redeemer and Friend.

We need to learn and relearn the details of his transcendent nature, the "God-ness of God." Let's take a closer look at some of his incommunicable attributes — those which we do not share with him, despite being made in his image. These are his independence, immutability, eternality, and omnipresence.

Independence

By his very nature, God is independent. Unlike us, his life and being do not depend on anything or anyone. When Moses asked God what he should be called, God replied, "I AM WHO I AM" (Exodus 3:14). In other words, he is both self-existent and self-sufficient.

In his best-selling book *The God Delusion*, pop atheist Richard Dawkins repeatedly asks the question: "Who made God?"[5] He and his colleagues proudly consider this the "unanswerable question" — an unbeatable ace of spades in their deadly gamble against faith. But their question merely misses the point. Dawkins assumes that something must have created the Creator because he cannot fathom the idea that anything could have existed outside of time forever. What if we creatures humbly yield to the truth that God is, in fact, the uncreated creator? Then, the senselessness of the question "Who made God?" becomes clear.

God was made from nowhere and by no one. He has always been.

John said of Jesus: "All things came into being through him, and apart from him nothing came into being that has come into being" (John 1:3 NASB). When the universe was birthed, it was created through God the Son. While God clearly has wants (that's why he created all things), he never experiences need. However, the whole of creation—planets, stars, beasts, people, Dawkins, me, and you—depends upon Christ who "upholds the universe by the word of his power" (Hebrews 1:3).

We are utterly dependent. God is magnificently not.

Eternality
God is also unlike us in that he has no beginning or end. He is in no way bound to the constructs of time.

Moses confessed in a prayer, "Before the mountains were brought forth, or ever you had formed the earth and the world, from everlasting to everlasting you are God" (Psalm 90:2). In other words, God is, has always been, and always will be.

The limit to God's existence is ... none. He calls himself both the *Alpha* and the *Omega*—the beginning and the end. A.W. Tozer observed, "The [human] mind looks backward in time till the dim past vanishes, then turns and looks into the future till thought and imagination collapse from exhaustion; and God is at both points, unaffected by either."[6] As the owner of time, nothing comes before him, nothing after.

God's eternality is good news and cause for worship. Whatever he is in attributes, nature, and divinity, he is eternally so. As the One who actually dwells in eternity, he is the only one who can guarantee eternal life.

Immutability

In his eternal being, God is immutable, or unchanging. This truth is critical to reverential worship: "For I the LORD do not change; therefore you, O children of Jacob, are not consumed" (Malachi 3:6). If we are to delight over God's majesty and splendor as they are displayed in his other attributes, then he must be unchanging. If God could ever come to a place of not being righteous, holy, or good, then we would be in big trouble, and our reverence toward him would be completely in vain.

Dutch theologian Herman Bavinck noted the importance of God's unchanging nature as it relates to his uniqueness from us (his God-ness):

The doctrine of God's immutability is of the highest significance for religion. The contrast between being and becoming marks the difference between the Creator and the creature. Every creature is continually becoming. It is changeable, constantly striving, seeks rest and satisfaction, and finds this rest in God, in him alone, for only he is pure being and no becoming. Hence, in Scripture God is often called the Rock. [7]

As an unmovable Rock, ours is a God who can be

trusted to keep his promises. He proved it with the substitutionary sacrifice of Jesus. He will also prove it when he comes to judge the living and the dead.

Because God is unchanging, there will never be an instant when he ceases to be worthy of reverential fear.

Omnipresence

Lewis said, "We may ignore, but we can nowhere evade, the presence of God. The world is crowded with him."[8] Not only does God exist in himself, without change, and at all times, he also exists in all places. David understood this when he wrote Psalm 139:

> Where shall I go from your Spirit?
>   Or where shall I flee from your presence?
> If I ascend to heaven, you are there!
>   If I make my bed in Sheol, you are there!
> If I take the wings of the morning
>   and dwell in the uttermost parts of the sea,
> even there your hand shall lead me,
>   and your right hand shall hold me.
> (Psalm 139:7-10)

Neither land nor sea, neither heaven nor hell: there is no flight from God's presence. Moreover, God sees and knows every one of our motives, deeds, and thoughts:

- "And no creature is hidden from his sight, but all are naked and exposed to the eyes of him to whom we must give account" (Hebrews 4:13).

- "And if you call on him as Father who judges impartially according to each one's deeds, conduct yourselves with fear throughout the time of your exile" (1 Peter 1:17).

We may try to fool others about what we are truly like; at times, we may even succeed. But there's no deceiving God. He is in all places and knows all things. When you remember your perpetual position before the presence of his fearsome majesty, all your sin simultaneously exposed yet lovingly robed in Christ's righteousness, then true humility and a spirit of repentance will seize your soul, and you will worship.

Do you see that God is not like us? Do you see the "God-ness" of God in his attributes? Does it humble you to glimpse the humanness of humanity? God is independent, immutable, eternal, and omnipresent. At our wisest, most inspired, and most insightful, we barely scrape the surface of his splendor and wonder. The list of his perfections goes on and on. God is not like us. Understanding this will only amplify for us the scandalous magnitude of his love, mercy, and infinite grace.

The Holiness of God

There is one attribute that Scripture uses to refer to God more often than any other. It is an attribute that, once we concede to it, reforms our understanding of all the others. This attribute is *holiness*. Our God is the Holy One.

What does Scripture mean when it says that God is holy?

A common mistake is to think of God's holiness largely in the human sense of the term. We can easily imagine that holiness is an abstract virtue by which things can be ranked and graded, with cheaters, murderers, and plunderers at one end of the scale and philanthropists, missionaries, and faithful clergy at the other. But if you imagine a perfect score on the "holy scale" as being 100, then I have a suggestion: start your imagination at 10,000, go up the scale as fast as possible, forever, and you might be about halfway to God's level of holiness.

The point, obviously, is that the holiness of God is simply off the charts. He is the perfection of all good. According to Scripture, God's holiness cannot be placed in the same category or scale as ours. It is *other*.

The very otherness of God, the true God-ness of God, means that he is completely separate from all that is not God. There is an infinite qualitative difference between him and us. "There is none besides you," declared Samuel (1 Samuel 2:2). There is no higher reality or virtue to which God must conform. There is no higher standard, or scale, by which he must be measured. He is not holy because he keeps the Law; the Law is holy because it reveals God. God is the only absolute. Everything else derives from him.

"I am God and not a man, the Holy One in your midst" (Hosea 11:9) His holiness is his unique, divine essence, and it is determined by no one. God in his holiness simply *is*. He deserves to be feared in reverential worship because he is holy. He is completely perfect, transcendent, and set apart in every way.

There is an eternal song of worship that appears

throughout the Bible, and it begins with the words "Holy, holy, holy" (Isaiah 6:3; Revelation 4:8). R. C. Sproul comments on this in his classic *The Holiness of God:*

> On a handful of occasions the Bible repeats something to the third degree. To mention something three times in succession is to elevate it to the superlative degree ....
>
> Only once in sacred Scripture is an attribute of God elevated to the third degree. The Bible says that God is holy, holy, holy .... The Bible never says that God is love, love, love; or mercy, mercy, mercy; or wrath, wrath, wrath; or justice, justice, justice.[9]

We need to get this. Is God loving? Of course. Is he merciful and just? Absolutely. But if we want to know anything truthful about God's love, mercy, or justice, then we need to start with his transcendent holiness. And that means we need to start with godly fear.

Why is a proper appreciation of God's holiness important to the fear of the Lord? Because that is where you must begin in order for your theology to conform to Scripture, which basically describes God's holiness as the umbrella over all his other attributes. If you begin with a statement like, "I believe God is love," and interpret all things through that filter, your view of God will fall tragically short and you will end up unable to imagine a God whose infinite holiness demands infinite punishment. If you begin with a statement like, "I believe God is just," and interpret all else through that filter, you'll end up unable to imagine a God whose infinite holiness was truly and completely satisfied by the infinite sacrifice of God the Son.

With our finite minds and limited souls, our human views of love, justice, and mercy are always inadequate and inconsistent. A man-based, "downward up" approach to trying to understand God will always fall horribly short, and leave us with insufficient and misleading conclusions. What we need to do is begin with the holiness of God. Interpreting the attributes of God from this "God downward" approach will fuel our fear of the Lord and intimately inform our worship and love for our Maker and Savior.

Stephen Charnock said "the holiness of God is his glory."[10] It is the measure of his enduring value. Charnock continued his thoughts on God's holiness, which we might also consider his purity, in this way:

> If every attribute of the Deity were a distinct member, purity would be the form, the soul, the spirit to animate them. Without it, his patience would be an indulgence to sin, his mercy a fondness, his wrath a madness, his power a tyranny, his wisdom an unworthy subtlety. It is this gives decorum to all.[11]

Someday God will destroy every competing glory and make his holiness known to every creature. But there is no need to wait for this. Learn, relearn, and remember that God is unlike us — set apart — in the most magnificent of ways. He is ever-present, authoritative, powerful, revered, and fearsome. Above all, he is holy. He alone is worthy of our praise.

Three
FEARSOME JUSTICE

During college I worked full-time in loss prevention for a large music retailer. For me it was a dream job. Commanding those five "eye in the sky" cameras, I could survey every inch of the retail floor. My job was to keep my eyes locked on the monitors to help prevent company losses, panning, tilting, and zooming the surveillance so I could watch everyone, employees and customers alike.

The best part was spotting shoplifters—it was almost literally a dream come true. You see, as a kid, I dreamed perpetually about being a vigilante crime-busting superhero. I *knew* there was a Batman-esque persona inside me somewhere just waiting to emerge. Fifteen years later, he showed up. From the secret lair of my control room, I had become the iron fist of justice, mysterious and invisible, yet omniscient and inescapable.

Watching shoplifters through surveillance cameras is fascinating. You wouldn't believe how often these adrenaline-pumped, would-be thieves look directly at the cameras, and then—what, having decided it didn't really look like anyone was watching? — grab the merchandise with trembling hands and tuck it away somewhere. I would shake my head and alert the security guards, and they would bring my prey into a small room where we would generally have a very predictable conversation.

"What were you thinking?" I would ask astonishedly.

"I guess I wasn't really thinking ... except about how much I wanted the CD."

"You looked right at me, you know. You looked right at the camera, and still decided you wanted it that badly?"

"I didn't think anyone was there. I just wanted it."

In a self-exalting moment of want, external authority was rejected. *There's nobody behind that camera. The only eyes here are my own. They see what I want, and I will take what they see as mine.*

Similar sentiments are expressed in the closing scenes of Ayn Rand's 1943 novel, *The Fountainhead*. Fictional hero Howard Roark had agreed to design an upscale housing project in exchange for complete anonymity and an agreement that his design would not be changed. Instead, the architect with whom he made the agreement put his own name on the project and changed the design, pushing Roark to demolish the building in a fit of revenge.

Roark, in the closing statements of his own defense, claimed he alone had the right to determine what was right for himself and anything he created:

> No creator was prompted by a desire to serve his brothers, for his brothers rejected the gift he offered and that gift destroyed the slothful routine of their lives.

His truth was his only motive. His own truth, and his own work to achieve it in his own way . . . . He held his truth above all things and against all men.
His vision, his strength, his courage came from his own spirit. A man's spirit, however, is his self . . . . To think, to feel, to judge, to act are functions of the ego . . . .
And only by living for himself was he able to achieve the things which are the glory of mankind.[12]

Rand's Howard Roark and the shoplifters I met have something in common. In their self-exaltation, they deem themselves as High Adjudicator of all that is right and true. Who is sovereign? Who calls the shots? Whose dominion is this? In these moments, they would answer, "I am in charge." *Me. Mine. Now.* This is their mantra. When you and I sin, it's our mantra, too.

The problem, of course, is that there is only one Judge—only one who sits on the throne of heaven. He is Yahweh, the only true and great I AM.

This very name God gave Moses for himself—Yahweh—demands our attention. Our English Bibles translate this name as *I AM* in Exodus 3. And *LORD* (in small caps) each time thereafter.

Read Psalm 135:5-6 with *Yahweh* everywhere your translation has *LORD* and think about how it describes God as judge over all:

For I know that Yahweh is great,
    and that our Lord is above all gods.
Whatever Yahweh pleases, he does,

in heaven and on earth,
in the seas and all deeps.

Only Yahweh is great and above all gods. After all, he self-existently *is*. From the heavens to the deep, only he can do as he pleases. The throne of High Judge is his, and there is no room for another; that seat is not meant for sharing.

What happens when created beings rebel against their Maker? It doesn't go well.

You Don't Mess With Yahweh

It's not exactly a popular statement: "Don't mess with God." Such sentiments are seen as archaic—too old-school, too fire-and-brimstone for this enlightened age. But if we listen carefully to the words of the Bible, we will hear over and over this undeniable anthem of God's fearsome justice. If we cannot hear, the problem is not in the telling but in the willingness to listen. Such willful deafness is never a good idea.

Take, for example, the fall of man. A crafty creature, the serpent seeks to subvert the created order and tempts the woman, Eve, instead of her husband, Adam. Eve succumbs, surrenders to temptation, eats, and then further assaults the goodness of God by offering the fruit to her husband. Adam foolishly eats as well.

The first man and woman chose to disobey the great I AM. They opted for self-will and sin. They subverted God's definition of good and tried to replace it with their own fatally flawed definition. Or to use the words of Proverbs 1:29, "they hated knowledge and did not choose the fear of the LORD." Among the three creatures in Genesis 3 — Adam, Eve, and the serpent — not one gave credence to the power and dominion of their Creator. And almost as soon as the fruit passes their lips, Adam and Eve's eyes open to the scandal of it all. God's image-bearers have defiled his very image with their sin. Ashamed, they hide to cover their nakedness, as if that will help; they fool no one. What happens next? Enter the Lord their Maker, God, and Provider. By virtue of his supreme faithfulness to defend all that is good, he is swift to exercise justice.

"Because you have done this," he tells the serpent, "you are cursed" (see Genesis 3:14). One day this crafty creature's skull will be crushed. [13]

God then evicts the man and the woman from the garden. Faithful to his word that disobeying his command would mean punishment by death outside of the garden's safety, Adam, Eve, and the countless generations that would follow are exiled into a fallen world, exposed to the terrors of sickness, suffering, sin, and death.

"Because you have sinned, the ground is cursed," he tells Adam (Genesis 3:17-18). Even the soil would groan from Adam's fall. It was a fearful day for our first parents. What is more, the holy judgment of justice that fell upon the garden that day has been reverberating through the corridors of history even to this day. Death. Sickness. Suffering. Groaning. All because of a single sin against the LORD our God.

When we turn the pages of history from that moment forward, we learn that Adam's sin was just the beginning; man's descent into sin continued without relent. By Genesis 6:5, we see that "the wickedness of man was great in the earth, and that every intention of the thoughts of his heart was only evil continually." The fear of God was suppressed by man's thirst for the ungodly. How does Yahweh respond to this rebellion? He sends a flood. Grieving over the folly of his creatures, he blots out and destroys every living person, save for one family preserved as an act of grace.

The story continues. Later in Genesis, we learn of two entire cities that were neck-deep in sexual immorality (18:29). Sodom and Gomorrah got rained on as well, this time with fire and sulfur from the heavens (Genesis 19:28). In the New Testament, Jude calls this an "example of punishment by eternal fire" (v 7)—the LORD's fire of justice that can never be quenched.

Beyond Genesis, we learn more of man's ongoing depravity and God's consequent judgment. In Exodus, we read of how Pharaoh and the Egyptians began oppressing God's chosen people, holding them in slavery for hundreds of years. God defends his people and judges his enemies by sending plagues—bloody rivers, a flood of frogs, dead livestock, skin disease, gnats, flies, hail, locusts, darkness. The LORD's final crushing blow? The life of every firstborn in every home not surrendered to him. "And there was a great cry in Egypt, for there was not a house where someone was not dead" (Exodus 12:30).

Imagine living as a slave in that town on that night. You hear the howls of lament from your neighbors. Your family is safe, as are the rest of Yahweh's people, but the mighty power of your God is made evident on that night.

It is a chilling time. You neither boast nor celebrate—you worship before the majesty, power, and sovereign grace of the great I AM. You worship with holy fear.

Some might say that God is not like this anymore, that he is no longer a God who sends floods, exiles families, and kills the firstborn. They might say that the New Testament God has evolved beyond this. He is more a kindly Father than a Divine Ruler on the throne. I actually once heard a young pastor teach this. From the pulpit, he declared that "God is not angry with his creatures anymore!" He then challenged us to find an angry God anywhere in the New Testament, insisting that such a God could not be found among its pages. I was shocked and saddened. To diminish the scope of God's judgment is to diminish the scope of his grace. Looking back, I regret that I didn't seize the moment and challenge him. I may have been hoping that he was going to correct himself, but, sadly, he did not. His assessment of God in the New Testament was dead wrong.

Judgment in the New Testament

In Acts 5, we read of Ananias and Sapphira, a husband-and-wife team of swindlers who selfishly cheat their church. What does God do? He strikes them dead. Scripture tells us that "great fear came upon the whole church and upon all who heard of these things" (Acts 5:11).

No kidding.

What about Jesus? Isn't he all mercy and grace? At the end of his Sermon on the Mount, Jesus warns that there are those who will approach him on the day of judgment,

confidently commending their good works and prophe-
cies before him, yet the Savior will greet them with, "I
never knew you; depart from me" (Matthew 7:21-23).

In Luke, Jesus warns his friends: "do not fear those
who kill the body, and after that have nothing more that
they can do" (12:5). He then exhorts them to instead "fear
him who, after he has killed, has authority to cast into hell"
(Luke 12:5). Apparently, Jesus believed that God has the
authority both to end the lives of human beings and then
to judge them.

Peter taught that Jesus is that God-appointed, almighty
"*judge* of the living and the dead" (Acts 10:42b). Moreover, in
Revelation, we see Jesus at work in a sobering and gruesome
glimpse of final judgment as the world is harvested and
many are thrown "into the great winepress of the wrath of
God" (14:19). We're told that out of the winepress pours a
184-mile pool of blood (Revelation 14:14-20). G. K. Beale
notes that this moment of "God's destruction of the impious
is as thoroughgoing as one mowing down the ripe harvest
and crushing grapes in the winepress." [14]

In the end, this divine judgment will continue in hell.
It will happen in the presence of the Lamb (Revelation
14:10), the mighty Savior and righteous Judge—not one
aspect of his character over the other, but both together.
Hell is not merely someplace empty of good, although it
will certainly be that. Nor will it be removed from God's
presence in the slightest. God, the risen Lamb, will indeed
be present; his grace, however, will not be.

This is the beloved God of the New Testament, just as
fearsome as Yahweh in the Old Testament. He is the same

faithful and unchanging defender of holiness throughout all 66 books of the Bible—the same yesterday, today, forever.

What Do We Make of This?

How do we respond to a God like this? Is he still loving? Is he still gracious? Can I approach him?

The short answer is yes, we can know with unwavering assurance that God is still loving and gracious. His Word tells us this, and we can trust it. But I suspect there are some who, after reading these accounts in Scripture, would disagree, merely seeing further support for their assumption that God is neither good nor worthy of holy fear. Instead, they might liken the God of the Bible to a totalitarian dictator or other narcissistic egomaniac. Atheists have told me that even if the resurrection were proved true, they would still reject Christianity because God is "wicked and unfair." They thumb their noses at the "atrocities" of the Old Testament and the judgment of the New. I know people who profess to be Christians, yet similarly reject the God of Scripture on these same bases and consider it absurd that any 21st century believer would ascribe to any doctrine of that old "fire and brimstone" sort.

But what if fire and brimstone is, in fact, a future reality for the damned? And what if it isn't God but, rather, we who are wicked and unfair? And what if his holy justice is, in fact, good?

We have been entranced with a low, man-obsessed view of sin since the fall of Adam. When men are removed from a blissful garden for eating forbidden fruit or struck dead for cheating their church family, the dilemma we ought to consider is not how small or great the sin is. The question to ask is, "How magnificent is the One who is sinned against?" When you and I sin against an infinitely holy God, then you and I are infinitely guilty and deserving of infinite destruction.

D. A. Carson elaborates on the magnitude of what we may consider "small" sin:

> It is the creature swinging his puny fist in the face of his Maker and saying, in effect, "If you do not see things my way, I'll make my own gods! I'll *be* my own god!" Small wonder that the sin most frequently said to arouse God's wrath is not murder, say, or pillage, or any other "horizontal" barbarism, but idolatry—that which dethrones God. That is why, in every sin, it is God who is the most offended party, as David himself well understood: "Against you, only, have I sinned and done what is evil in your sight; so you are right in your verdict and justified when you judge" (Psalm 51:4).[15]

God's judgment is not arbitrary, nor is it misguided. He is judge not because he's "judgmental" but because he is the supreme defender of all that is holy and good. His righteous wrath exists to uphold the demands of his moral law. His isn't a sinful, resentful, or militant zeal for glory; it is an impassioned zeal, driven by divine love for his perfect holiness.

Think about this: from one sin of one man an entire race's legacy is condemned. So look at the world around us. Look down the corridors of time. Just a cursory glance reveals the effects of this fall. Sin. Calamities. Perversion. Hatred. Suffering. Sickness. Cancer. Death. All ushered into this world by one man's *one sin*. Now, avert your eyes from the world around and consider what's within your own heart. How's the view? Does it look much better? If you're anything like me, the answer is no. I've committed thousands more sins than those recorded of Adam, and these are just the ones I'm aware of.

We are certainly a sinfully depraved people living under the dominion of an infinitely holy, majestic, powerful, and mighty God. So consider the holiness of God, the one who says of himself, "I AM WHO I AM." Do you feel any sense of helplessness at all? Any reverence? Any awe? If so, that is a glimmer of the fear of the Lord.

I hope you realize that it is impossible to have too high view of God. Don't worry about overdoing it in this area; there's no risk of that. And the higher our view of God the greater our recognition of how desperately we need a Savior.

The Bible tells us that each one of us will stand before the judgment seat of God one day. It could be today. It could be decades from now. Either way, we can be certain the day is coming (Romans 14:10). The impious have often scoffed at the idea of such a time. "If there's an afterlife, I'm going to ask God about [name your complaint here]."

No, you are not, my friend. There will be no asking. On the day of judgment, we return to stand before our Maker, where we would do well to remember Isaiah 29:16: "Shall the potter be regarded as the clay, that the thing made should say of its maker, 'He did not make me'; or the thing formed say of him who formed it, 'He has no understanding'"?

37

The most humbling thoughts I have ever had are of the day I will stand personally accountable before him. We're told his face will shine like the sun in full strength, his eyes flickering as flames, his feet as bronze, his tongue a two-edged sword, and his voice like the roar of many waters.

This will be no moment to offer complaints or demand explanations. There will only be worship: reverence, awe, wonder. Fear of the Lord. On that day, you and I will give credence to the judge of all the earth, acknowledging his dominion over us.

Don't ever abandon the fear of the Lord. You cannot mock the Lord our God. You cannot play games with him. I love the way the band Thrice expresses this in the song "Kings Upon the Main":[16]

> Despite the best of maps and the bravest men
> For all their mighty names and massive forms
> There'll never be, there has never been
> A ship or fleet secure against the storms
>
> When kings upon the main have clung to pride
> And held themselves as masters of the sea
> I've held them down beneath the crushing tide
> Till they have learned that no one masters me
>
> But grace can still be found within the gale
> With fear and reverence, raise your ragged sail

Is grace available for that day? Absolutely. His name is Jesus. He is the only surety we have.

Four
HOLY FEAR AND THE CROSS

We have seen that God is a fearsome defender of justice and holiness. We have seen that he is zealous for his glory and will not hesitate to punish all sin, and righteously so. We have seen that God can and does pour out wrath on sinners. And we have seen that when God exercises judgment, he does so to uphold his goodness, his holiness, his faithfulness, and his justice.

But we have yet to consider God's greatest, most extreme, and most severe act of judgment — one in which he upholds both justice and mercy, along with grace, love, hope, and life. In this act of judgment lies the only hope we have from the deserved wrath of God. I am thinking of the crucifixion of Jesus Christ.

In the cross, all things pertaining to man's salvation hold together beautifully. Justice and mercy meet as God and man are reconciled. And by that miracle of salvation a new possibility is created. Holy fear becomes no longer a matter of terror for us, but a matter of awe and wonder as we give credence to this amazing God of justice and mercy who has punished his own Son as a sacrifice for our sins. For the Christian, holy fear can create a glorious synergy between our acknowledgement of grace, our experience of gratitude, and our expression of worship.

Where Justice and Mercy Meet

We have seen that God hates sin as a scandalous offense against him and, as a result, all sin must ultimately be punished. In fact, every sin ever committed, from the Garden of Eden until the time of Christ's return, will be addressed in one of two ways. On behalf of those for whom Jesus died — whether living, passed on, or yet to be — sin *has been* punished in the eternally significant sacrifice of Christ on the cross. With respect to those who will never bow the knee to Jesus Christ as Lord and Savior, their sin will be punished eternally in hell. The horror and tragedy of that fact is perhaps the single most powerful indicator we have in all of Scripture of the infinite antagonism between sin and holiness, the magnitude of the gulf between God's purity and the pollution of sin.

So God is holy, but he is also just. He is full of grace and mercy, but he has never-ending wrath against sin. We speak of God's attributes individually as an aid to understanding him, and at times those attributes can seem inconsistent or even antagonistic to one another. Yet in practice, his many attributes ever and always complement one another. We must not imagine the justice of God as an absence of mercy, or the mercy of God as an absence of justice. Like all of God's attributes and ways, they coexist and work together, sometimes mysteriously, but always perfectly. Indeed, at the cross we witness justice and mercy acting in perfect union.

Hebrews 9 helps us begin to understand how this can happen. "Indeed, under the law almost everything is purified with blood, and without the shedding of blood there is no forgiveness of sins" (Hebrews 9:22). In order for sins to be forgiven (mercy), blood must be shed (justice). Whose blood? Is it our blood? No. Our blood would not purify us or merit forgiveness. The only blood that could forgive sins and secure salvation from God's wrath is the blood of imperishable worth—that of the Son of God.

How can the shed blood of the Son of God become effective for us? The answer involves *substitution* and *propitiation*.

Substitution. I can't play basketball the way I used to. My stamina on the court today would embarrass my 16-year-old self. I'm not out there too long before my knees start to creak and my lungs begin to ache. At that point, I'll happily let a substitute step in from the sidelines so I can rest. That's what "subs" do in most team sports. They take your place so that you can rest and regroup.

The Christian has a substitute of a far more valuable sort. His substitution is not simply for our temporal rest but for our eternal salvation. Nor did he merely engage in sport for us. Jesus suffered on the cross as "the righteous for the unrighteous" (1 Peter 3:18). He took upon himself the wrath of God in our place.

Propitiation. There's a biblical term for what happened on that cross, and its meaning is at the heart of the gospel. The term is *propitiation.*[17] "For all have sinned and fall short of the glory of God, and are justified by his grace as a gift, through the redemption that is in Christ Jesus, whom God put forward as a *propitiation by his blood*" (Romans 3:23-25). When the Bible says that Jesus was a propitiation for our sins, it means that he appeased the fullness of God's wrath on our behalf. He did not *deflect* God's wrath, as a baseball bat deflects a baseball or my high block deflects your judo chop. Rather, the Son of God *absorbed* God's holy and omnipotent wrath. He satisfied it. Romans 8:32 says that God "did not spare his own Son." In other words, the Father did not hold back. He let Jesus have it. The wrath that you and I so richly deserved, Jesus the Son so willingly received.[18] This is why we sing:

> Till on that cross as Jesus died,
> The wrath of God was satisfied;
> For ev'ry sin on Him was laid—
> Here in the death of Christ I live.[19]

On the other side of his death, we have life! Indeed, when Jesus Christ served as a propitiation by his blood, he took the omnipotent holy blow of God's wrath for us.

What an astonishing plan—the fearsome justice of God met fearsome mercy in Christ, a Savior who, although he truly and actually died, did not remain in the grave. Who among us could have imagined that the infinite and holy God would choose to save finite and sinful creatures through the death of his own Son? This is how God can fully maintain his justice and holiness while extending mercy and forgiveness to sinners. In the work of Christ on the cross, we see the wisdom of God on full display.

Paul uses the word "manifold" to describe God's wisdom in salvation, telling us that the eternal purpose of God's divine redemption plan is "that through the church the manifold wisdom of God might now be made known" (Ephesians 3:10). This word "manifold" is translated from the Greek *polypoikilos*, which appears only once in the New Testament—in this verse. It means "much variegated, marked with a great variety of colors." In other words, the wisdom of God in salvation is multifaceted in its splendor.

The Bible sheds more light in 1 Corinthians 1:22-24, where Paul writes, "For Jews demand signs and Greeks seek wisdom, but we preach Christ crucified, a stumbling block to Jews and folly to Gentiles, but to those who are called, both Jews and Greeks, Christ the power of God and the wisdom of God." The "manifold wisdom of God" was required to construct a plan that would unite and redeem sinners from every nation—Jew and Gentile— contrary to all human rationale, by the dreadful death of the mighty Messiah. Who else could devise such a God-exalting and man-humbling design?

At the cross, the righteous wrath of God met the merciful grace of God. Whether we are Jew or Gentile our hope, therefore, does not lie in further rebellion. It does not lie in our resolve. It does not lie in our work or our wisdom. Our only hope from the wrath of God is the grace of God, found only in the person and work of Jesus of Nazareth. By the shedding of Jesus' blood on the cross, the seemingly contradictory themes of God's love for holy justice and his love for wrath-deserving sinners are joined in one awesome union that displays the manifold wisdom of God.

This is undoubtedly part of the reason that Paul wrote, "I decided to know nothing among you except Jesus Christ and him crucified" (1 Corinthians 2:2). The gospel is more than just good news; it is the news to end all news. Is there anything else more worth knowing?

The Fuel and the Fruit of Holy Fear

If God's wrath is satisfied in Jesus, then is there still reason to fear the Lord? Yes! The grace of God does not replace the fear of God; if anything, it amplifies it.

When we have no fear of the Lord and do not acknowledge the power of our Maker, it seems that our sin is no gross offense. We imagine, then, that the Judge cannot be too upset about our sin, which means the Savior didn't really have to do very much for us; the sacrifice of his work on the cross is radically diminished. But when we see that the fear of the Lord is itself the very acknowledgment of God's power over us, and that this leads to a high view of both sin's offense and God's judgment against sin, we begin to grasp how the fear of God actually amplifies the grace of God.

The greater our godly fear, the more we hate our sin. And the more we hate our sin, the more we long for a Savior. Then, when we see that God has provided this salvation in "redemption that is in Christ Jesus, whom God put forward" (Romans 3:24-25), our gratitude for God's saving work is magnified. Godly and reverential fear will inevitably lead to godly and reverential worship.

At the same time, the grace of God, rightly understood, amplifies the fear of the Lord:

> If you, O LORD, should mark iniquities,
>   O Lord, who could stand?
> But with you there is forgiveness,
>   that you may be feared.
> (Psalm 130:3-4)

That's a peculiar phrase, isn't it? "With you there is forgiveness, *that* you may be feared." Just as godly fear produces a love of the gospel, so a love of the gospel produces godly fear. George Bowen explains:

> This forgiveness, this smile of God, binds the soul to God with a beautiful fear. Fear to lose one glance of love. Fear to lose one work of kindness. Fear to be carried away from the heaven of his presence by an insidious current of worldliness. Fear of slumber. Fear of error. Fear of not enough pleasing him. Our duty, then, is to drink deep of God's forgiving love. To be filled with it is to be filled with purity, fervency, and faith. Our sins have to hide their diminished heads, and slink away through crevices, when forgiveness — when Christ — enters the soul.[20]

What we believe informs how we live. If we really have our theology right, then the emotions that help undergird godly living will follow naturally. That is, if we truly understand godly fear, and if we truly understand the grace that is ours in the cross, we will naturally hate our sin, feel gratitude to God for his grace and mercy, and worship him for his goodness and kindness.

The union of God's judgment and God's mercy in the death of Jesus, whom God himself put forward, leaves no room for boasting, only for reverential worship. With godly fear, reverence for his judgment, and gratitude for his mercy, we can echo the doxology of Paul when he closed his wonderful treatise on the gospel: "to the only wise God be glory forevermore through Jesus Christ! Amen" (Romans 16:27).

Five
HOLY FEAR AND ITS BENEFITS

Do you see why the fear of the Lord is a doctrine we must not overlook? When godly fear informs our understanding of divine holiness, judgment, mercy, and wisdom, our God is revealed as fully worthy of reverential worship. The rest of this book will help us understand the differences between holy and unholy fear — godly and ungodly fear — so we can make right application in our own lives.

Jesus said that his followers could be identified by what their lives produce (Luke 6:43-45). The results of living with holy fear are different than the results of living with unholy fear. In the safety of God's care, for example, the God-fearer is given goodness (Psalm 31:19) and salvation (Luke 1:50). But the three benefits of living as a God-fearer most often mentioned in Scripture are wisdom, assurance, and delight.

Holy Fear Brings Wisdom

The single best place to begin to comprehend the relationship between wisdom and godly fear is Psalm 111:10,

"The fear of the LORD is the beginning of wisdom." That is to say, *anything pertaining to wisdom flows out of the fear of the Lord*; it is the first step to wise thinking and living. Do you want to think wisely? Fear God. Do you want to live wisely? Fear God. In the same way that a house needs a firm foundation, so does true wisdom need to be undergirded by godly fear.

How is it that we become wiser through godly fear? Here's one way to think about it that may be helpful. To worship God in the humility of holy fear, to believe and trust in him and his Word—these are themselves acts of wisdom. To believe God in this way, and to act on that belief, is to position ourselves to receive fresh grace and mercy from God. It is a form of calling out for wisdom, seeking it like silver (Proverbs 2:4), and God is eager to answer that request.

Proverbs 11:2 rounds out the idea by specifically bringing in the concepts of pride and humility: "When pride comes, then comes disgrace, but with the humble is wisdom." A man who is proud, as the serpent was proud, does not have a high view of God and does not fear him. But the God-fearing man has a low estimation of himself and a high view of God. Consequently, he will be humble as well as teachable. A tree of wisdom can grow many fruits when planted in the tender soil of godly fear.

The wisdom of the Word. The wisdom that God bestows on the one who regards him with holy fear also manifests itself in a love for God's Word, especially the authority of that Word. A friend once lamented to me that the church he attended was "too big on the Bible" and "too little about God." This is a false and dangerous dichotomy.

Beyond the eloquent but general revelation of nature, what hope do we have of knowing anything specific about a God whose ways are higher than our ways and whose thoughts are higher than our thoughts? How can we learn of his character, his ways, his commands? While there certainly are limits to what we can know about God, he has chosen his Word to provide us with all that we must know in order to honor and represent him and his gospel in the world.

Ever since God began to speak to his people corporately following the exodus from Egypt, the written word has been absolutely central. How important is this idea to God? *God's first written words to man were inscribed by his own finger* (Exodus 31:18; 32:16) and began with the eternal declaration, "I am the LORD your God" (Exodus 20:2). The tablets on which these words were written were later stored in the holiest place in all Israel, inside the ark of the covenant.

As the history of Israel unfolded, God sent additional prophets who further proclaimed his words in written form. Jesus himself affirmed the divine words of the Old Testament and appointed apostles who would likewise speak and write for God in the New Testament. Thus, in a very real sense, Scripture is the God of manifold wisdom writing to us. This is why, historically, the church has referred to the Bible as the Word of God.

In Deuteronomy 4:10, Moses recalls receiving from God his precious words on the stone tablets containing the Ten Commandments: "On the day that you stood before the Lord your God at Horeb, the Lord said to me, 'Gather the people to me, that I may let them hear my words, so that they may learn to fear me all the days that they live on the earth, and that they may teach their children so.'"

God told Moses clearly that we learn holy fear, as God would have us learn it, not by signs and wonders, but by words. Yes, on the day Moses received the Ten Commandments from God, the entire mountain was embraced by darkness, clouds, and gloom. Yet God's *words* are what taught them godly fear, and those same words passed on communicate holy fear to subsequent generations.

Any attempt at Christian spirituality that does not include at its heart a reverence for God's Word is vague at best. As God-fearing people, we must esteem his Word, believe what it says, and do what it commands.

- Do you want to know God? Read his Word.
- Do you want know things about him? See what his Word declares.
- Do you want to grow closer to God? Do what his Word says.
- Do you want to treasure Christ? Treasure him through his Word.

Immerse yourself in the Word of God. Search it. Savor it. It is more amazing than any technology, more true than any other book, more compelling than any film, more profound than any other insight or observation, more glorious than any sunset, more beautiful than any song, more probing than any human encounter. It is a double-edged sword forged under the weight of God's voice—the voice that birthed the universe—and it judges the very thoughts and intentions of our hearts (Hebrews 4:12).

The wisdom of obedience. To live under the authority of God and his Word necessarily means to live in obedience to him. As John Bunyan said, "It is not the knowledge of the will of God, but our sincere complying therewith, that proveth we fear the Lord."[21] When we fear the Lord, we let the Word of the Lord forge our desires and fashion our values.

Proverbs 16:6 says something similar: "by the fear of the LORD one turns away from evil." This is not a turning from sin out of slavish fear. Recall our definition of fear. Rather, it is *giving credence* to the Father of justice, mercy, wisdom, and power. We turn from sin out of godly fear because we know and trust that it is the better choice in every way, and the choice that pleases the Father. Charles Bridges writes,

> The implanted principle of obedience is no legal bondage. The fear of the Lord is at once a bridle to sin, and a spur to holiness. It changes the slave into a child. Filial confidence—its twin-grace—covers from sin. [Sin's] very touch is hateful; and all its ways are abhorred and forsaken.[22]

As adopted children of God, then, we look to the only begotten Son as our model for how we should relate to our heavenly Father. The scandal of the gospel—that the Son was punished for our sins—is a great fuel for obedience, one made all the more powerful by godly fear. So the apostle Peter exhorted the "elect exiles" who "call on [God] as Father":

> Conduct yourselves with fear throughout the time of your exile, knowing that you were ransomed from the futile ways inherited from your forefathers, not with perishable things such as silver or gold, but with the precious blood of Christ, like that of a lamb without blemish or spot. He was foreknown before the foundation of the world but was made manifest in the last times for your sake, who through him are believers in God, who raised him from the dead and gave him glory, so that your faith and hope are in God. (1 Peter 1:17-21)

As we mentioned in the previous chapter, this good news of God's grace is not opposed to the fear of the Lord (holy credence). If anything, it is reason for it! We have been ransomed from the grips of depravity—a helpless state—by the blood of the Lamb who will judge the living and the dead. Christians can fear (and thus obey) God *because* we know the value of the precious, priceless, powerful blood of Christ by which we were ransomed.

This obedience that grows out of a holy fear of the Lord is always active, never passive. There are certainly "holding pattern" times in the Christian life, during which we continue praying and believing while we wait for God to move in some area, but these times are clearly different from laziness and inactivity. Paul reminds his readers in Philippians 2:13, "as you have always obeyed … *work out* your salvation with *fear and trembling*, for it is God who works in you, both to will and to work for his good pleasure."

Obedience done in wisdom recognizes that, on the one hand, our perseverance does not depend on us—it is God's work—but on the other hand, we must never sit slothfully without resolve and wait for God to carry us through. As D. A. Carson notes, "Paul tells us to work out our salvation with fear and trembling, *precisely because* God is working in us both to will and to act according to his good purpose …. He works in us at the level of our wills and at the level of our doing." [23]

Paul's language in Philippians 2 is insistent. Because you know this mighty and wonderful God, work out your salvation. Work it out with the kind of holy fear that leaves you trembling before his awesome holiness. In this way, you will live to please your Maker.

Holy Fear Brings Assurance

What is all our hope and peace? Nothing but the blood of Jesus.

In the quote from 1 Peter 1 in the previous section, did you notice what Peter said would be the ultimate fruit of reverential living and treasuring of the gospel? He said it is "so that your faith and hope are in God" (1 Peter 1:21).

The God-fearing man who values the precious blood of Jesus is also the man who knows his security could lie in no other.

When I found myself helplessly stuck beneath the pull of a rip tide with no one to save me, I knew that my only hope from the power of the ocean was, in a sense, the power of the ocean. God in his mercy intervened and turned the power of the ocean from being my executioner to being my savior. It is the same with God himself. When we were helpless and headed for death under God's irresistible power, he had mercy. His infinite divine power that would have inevitably ensured our eternal condemnation now inevitably ensures our eternal blessing. God can and does keep us eternally secure in our deliverance from his judgment.

Many believe that once a person is saved by the power of God, it is then up to other forces to keep him or her in God's favor. The Roman Catholic Church, for example, has historically taught that sin comes in two varieties: mortal and venial. The first is so grave that the Christian can lose his God-given grace because of it; the latter is a lesser sin that is reparable by acts of penance. Similar views are present within much of Protestant Christianity. All these are legalistic perspectives that rely on human performance to maintain God's favor. They stem from a low view of God and a meager appreciation of sin's wretchedness.

In contrast, the fear of the Lord reminds us that hope in this life and the next lies not in our own will, but in the will and provision of the great I AM, the God who "put

[Christ] forward" (Romans 3:25) also "raised him from the dead and gave him glory, so that your faith and our hope are in God" (1 Peter 1:21).

If men are as a vapor (James 4:14) and Christ is as a rock (Acts 4:11), which would you rather have serving as your foundation?

In the words of a great hymn:

> My hope is built on nothing less
> Than Jesus' blood and righteousness;
> I dare not trust the sweetest frame,
> But wholly lean on Jesus' Name.
> On Christ the solid Rock, I stand;
> All other ground is sinking sand.[24]

Where does our confidence lie? Where is our hope? *Who* is our hope? In his letter, Jude warned his readers of false teachers who had snuck into their ranks unnoticed, saying these teachers would suffer judgment under God's hand (Jude 4). Likely anticipating that these readers might then begin to question their own security, he closed his letter with this wonderful doxology: "Now to him who is able to keep you from stumbling and to present you blameless before the presence of his glory with great joy, to the only God, our Savior, through Jesus Christ our Lord, be glory, majesty, dominion, and authority, before all time and now and forever. Amen" (Jude 24-25).

Those are strong words: "to him who is able." Jude's short letter shows that our God is able both to "execute judgment on all" (v 15) and to preserve the "beloved in

God" (v 1). We have a fearsome God! And we can be assured of his faithfulness to preserve all he has called through the preaching of the gospel. What God began, he will be faithful to complete (Philippians 1:6). Rest assured.

Holy Fear Brings Delight

At a trying time in my life, the Lord used Isaiah 11 to minister to my soul. Prophesying of the Messiah, Isaiah wrote these divinely inspired words:

> And the Spirit of the LORD shall rest upon him,
>> the Spirit of wisdom and understanding,
>> the Spirit of counsel and might,
>> the Spirit of knowledge and the fear of the LORD.
> And his delight shall be in the fear of the LORD.
> (Isaiah 11:2-3)

I thought it was a curious marriage of words *delight* and *fear*. But there you have it—Jesus himself would *delight* in the *fear* of the LORD. Nehemiah 1:11 presses the point further, "O Lord, let your ear be attentive to the prayer of your servant, and to the prayer of your servants who delight to fear your name." There it is again. Not just the Son of God, but the people of God also find delight in fearing him.

Delight and fear together? This can only be explained by a burning love for beholding God in all his splendor and majesty. John Piper says we were made to do just that:

> We are all starved for the glory of God, not self. No

one goes to the Grand Canyon to increase self-esteem. Why do we go? Because there is greater healing for the soul in beholding splendor than there is in beholding self. Indeed, what could be more ludicrous in a vast and glorious universe like this than a human being, on the speck called earth, standing in front of a mirror trying to find significance in his own self-image?[25]

We are made to behold the glory of Another. Focus on self and your world turns inward, growing continually smaller, duller, and more isolated. But a God-entranced vision of the whole of life opens up the soul to endless God-glorifying wonders and evokes a profound sense of divine majesty and grace. It produces joyful and reverential fear, breathtaking awe, and a selfless brokenness and humility that radiates the beauty of he who was humble enough to die for sinners.

To fear the Lord as a Christian is to give credence to the awesome power by which God saves us — the shattering realization that although we deserve eternal death, we have been given eternal life. Why would we not have joy and delight in that fear?

May we never look for wisdom, assurance, or delight from any other source. As the psalmist Asaph confessed, "Whom have I in heaven but you? And there is nothing on earth that I desire besides you" (Psalm 73:25)

Wisdom, assurance, and delight. These are just a few of the immeasurable benefits of embracing the holy fear of a loving, omnipotent God.

Six

UNHOLY FEAR AND ITS CAUSES

Ever since the Garden, unholy fear has haunted mankind. Indeed, *holy* fear of the Lord is only possible for two types of people: Christians, and unbelievers whom God is giving a glimpse of himself. Yet even for Christians who are daily trying to walk in ways that honor Christ, unholy fear can be a frequent temptation.

Just as a Christian can still sin, we can get stuck in unholy fear, which tells us to flee from God and seek some other salvation. God knows this is an ongoing struggle for us, so among many other helps he has given us 1 John 4:18: "There is no fear in love, but perfect love casts out fear. For fear has to do with punishment, and whoever fears has not been perfected in love."

It is important to see that John's purpose in this verse is not to distinguish between holy and unholy fear. In fact, he is using *fear* as shorthand for *unholy fear*. We know this because the full counsel of Scripture clearly teaches that there *is* holy fear in love, and that perfect love does not cast out *holy* fear but actually makes it stronger.

In fact, I believe we do no violence to Scripture if we simply replace the general word *fear* in this verse with the more specific concept of *unholy fear*: "There is no unholy fear in love, but perfect love casts out unholy fear. For unholy fear has to do with punishment, and whoever experiences unholy fear has not been perfected in love."

John was passing this wisdom along to Christians because they needed to hear it. We need to hear it, too. Many of our day-to-day fears reveal a lack of trust in God. This is the fear that frets and sweats over countless things both great and small. It furrows its brow and wrings its hands, constantly wondering, "Am I safe? Am I secure?" Unholy fear makes us feel trapped, claustrophobic, ever walking the knife-edge of danger.

Common Causes of Unholy Fear

There are at least three common causes of unholy fear among Christians:

- A faulty understanding of God
- A faulty understanding of God's finished work
- A faulty understanding of God's ongoing work

Unholy fear misunderstands God. Unholy fear makes a tyrant out of God, turning a blind eye to his goodness and giving credence only to his judgment. This is the fear that drove Adam to hide. It is also the fear epitomized by the wicked and slothful servant in the parable of the talents who apparently mischaracterized his master when he said, "Master, I knew you to be a hard man, reaping where you did not sow, and gathering where you scattered no seed" (Matthew 25:24).

When we consider the revelation God has given of himself, we can clearly see what a false picture of God that is. Scripture is full of God's holiness and justice *and* mercy and goodness. We must recall that God's justice and mercy meet in perfect union at the cross for our good and for his glory.

To misunderstand the fullness of God's character is to be crippled in the Christian life. As Thomas Manton writes,

> This was the fear of the slothful servant in the text; and such a fear have many others in the bosom of their hearts, by which they can never do anything effectually in the business of religion, by reason of their strong prejudices, occasioned by their own tormenting fear.[26]

Unholy fear misunderstands what God has done.
Unholy fear tells us that the propitiatory work Christ accomplished on the cross was not enough to justify us before God. This type of fear drives us to make endless efforts at pleasing God through merit, giving, charity, and legalism. It is like building a second foundation of human works upon the perfect foundation of Jesus' divine work, as if his was not enough. Instead of letting our good works flowing *out of* our position in Christ, we attempt to gather good works *into* our position in Christ. This lowers God and his work and exalts our own. To Paul, this was an alarming offense:

I am astonished that you are so quickly deserting him who called you in the grace of Christ and are turning to a different gospel—not that there is another one, but there are some who trouble you and want to distort the gospel of Christ. But even if we or an angel from heaven should preach to you a gospel contrary to the one we preached to you, let him be accursed. (Galatians 1:6-8)

Two chapters later, Paul clarifies the specifics of their offense:

O foolish Galatians! Who has bewitched you? It was before your eyes that Jesus Christ was publicly portrayed as crucified. Let me ask you only this: Did you receive the Spirit by works of the law or by hearing with faith? Are you so foolish? Having begun by the Spirit, are you now being perfected by the flesh? (Galatians 3:1-3)

We might be tempted to think that Paul, who calls the Galatian church *brothers* in chapter 1, was being a tad harsh when he called them fools—twice! But Paul was genuinely concerned for them and for what their error said about their understanding of God's work. Paul loved this church deeply. His confrontation was not in spite of his love for them but because of it. Gripped by the unholy fear of partial justification, the church in Galatia had slipped into legalistic moralism and was subverting the gospel of God's sovereign grace.

Unholy fear doubts what God can and will do.
Jesus seems to draw a direct correlation between unholy
fear and a demonstrated lack of faith: "Why are you afraid,
O you of little faith?" (Matthew 8:26). When Christ
wanted to rid his disciples of unholy fear, he rebuked them
for their lack of faith.

Most of us have experienced unholy fear kicking in
when times get tough. Yet it is in these moments when we
should most cling to God, even run to him. "I have fled
to you for refuge!" (Psalm 143:9), wrote David. When
we doubt God's faithfulness, we do not seek the refuge
we so desperately need, and we rob our souls of the help
that God's promises so abundantly provide. Instead of
running to him for refuge, we scramble for our own help.

Unholy fear is also in evidence whenever we begin to
envy the world. The psalmist Asaph understood this well
when he penned the grumbling beginning of Psalm 73:

> I was envious of the arrogant
>> when I saw the prosperity of the wicked ....
> Their eyes swell out through fatness;
>> their hearts overflow with follies ....
>> always at ease, they increase in riches.
> All in vain have I kept my heart clean
>> and washed my hands in innocence.
> (Psalm 73:3,7,12)

So here's Asaph envious, bitter, and discontent over
the material prosperity of unbelievers. He considers this
highly "unfair," and it provokes the green-eyed monster

within. He is doing exactly what you and I have done—measuring God's faithfulness by our personal material circumstances.

Defining the Two Fears

How do we really tell, in a particular situation, if a fear we face is holy or unholy? To me, Charles Spurgeon offers the simplest, cleanest, most useful distinction when he talks about holy fear driving us to God and unholy fear driving us away. In other words, holy fear says, "Whatever else may be going on, no matter how bad it looks, I know my salvation in this situation lies in God." Unholy fear says, "God can't or won't help you with *this* problem—at least, not in the way you might prefer—so you had better find some other savior, some other means of escape."

Let's look at the difference between holy and unholy fear from several slightly different angles to try to round out the picture:

- Holy fear compels us to run to God as our only hope. Unholy fear drives us away from God and toward whatever false savior seems close at hand.
- Holy fear is the relationship of a child to a good and loving father. Unholy fear is the relationship of servant or slave to an unkind and unpredictable master.
- Holy fear is based in a family relationship that you treasure and wants to cultivate. Unholy fear is based in a merely legal relationship that you dislike but cannot escape.

- Holy fear sees God as your Father who is loving and omnipotent. Unholy fear sees God as either not Father, not loving, and/or not omnipotent.

Holy fear acknowledges the awesome power that God has over us, but that acknowledgment is informed by the knowledge that we are his beloved children. Holy fear rules over all other fears and sends us running to the Lord as our only true hope.

The Way of Escape

Understanding the difference between the two fears will go a great distance to give us the tools we need to move away from unholy fear and toward holy fear. Godly fear reminds us that God is bigger, more powerful, and more trustworthy than any circumstance our fallen world has to offer. It reminds us that God's provision in Jesus was great enough to justify us before him. It reminds us that his mercy is great enough that we may safely run to him and rightfully expect him to welcome us with open arms. It reminds us that God is faithful to his character and his promises. Godly fear reminds us that God is our only hope.

Asaph finally realized this about halfway through Psalm 73 when he wrote, "But when I thought how to understand [the prosperity of the wicked], it seemed to me a wearisome task, until I went in to the sanctuary of God; then I discerned their end" (Psalm 73:17).

What happens in a sanctuary? You meet God. You draw near to him. You behold him for who he is. And you worship. The remedy for all sinful fear is reminding ourselves who God is, what he has done, and what he will do, so that we might turn to him in worship.

The fear of the LORD is the beginning of wisdom. And by his grace and provision, that fear is ours for the taking. Seize it and worship him alone.

Seven
THE SNARE OF FEARING MAN

When I was in high school, I had a common idol: I worshiped my own image in the eyes of others. I tried baggy clothes, shell necklaces, bleached hair, and pierced ears. I begged my parents to let me have a pager (this was actually cool at the time). No deal, and I was outraged when a younger friend got one before I did. In my junior year, I ran for class secretary without having the slightest clue what a class secretary was or did. I just knew I'd get an extra picture in the yearbook. Pathetic, I know.

The Bible has a diagnosis for this condition: the fear of man. Proverbs 29:25 says, "The fear of man lays a snare," and I know that's true because I was trapped in it—caught and held tight. Few things can get a firmer grip on the human heart than the fear of man.

Ed Welch has a helpful book on this topic called *When People Are Big and God Is Small*. In it, he writes,

> The fear of man can be summarized this way: We replace God with people. Instead of a biblically

guided fear of the Lord, we fear others … .
When we are in our teens, it is called "peer pressure."
When we are older, it is called "people-pleasing."
Recently, it has been called "codependency." With
these labels in mind, we can spot the fear of man
everywhere.[27]

Under this helpful definition, I would venture to say
we must all plead guilty.

Fearing Your Position before Men

The fear of man is a manifestation of pride, as common
and widespread a sin as there is. How does fear of man
manifests itself for you?

Are you a bona fide people-pleaser? A yes-man?
Do you care a little too much what other people think
about you? What they say about you? Perhaps you
avoid conflict at all costs. Perhaps you crave recognition—secretly or not so secretly. Maybe you fish for
compliments, gossip about or judge others in order to
feel better about yourself, or strive to be more politically
correct than biblically correct. If so, you might have a fear
of man issue, and it's high time to call it what it is: sin.

When we fear our position before men, we worship
the creature rather than the Creator. This is textbook
idolatry, plain and simple. In practice, however, most of
us would sooner offend God than someone we know.
We forget the chilling words of our Lord, "For whoever
is ashamed of me and of my words in this adulterous

and sinful generation, of him will the Son of Man also be ashamed when he comes in the glory of his Father with the holy angels" (Mark 8:38).

Whose approval do you most desire when you work your job? When you serve at church? When you volunteer for needs? Do you seek to please people more than you do God? It's a powerful snare, often tricky, so watch your step.

Several years back, I got a call from someone on staff at the church. The following week, the church was planning to take a group of about 50 of us college students to a conference retreat in the mountains. The woman on the phone asked if I'd be willing to share with the group for ten minutes on why a personal prayer life is important. I knew most everyone in our group, so I thought, "No big deal," and gladly agreed. Little did I know that she was actually referring to the entire conference of 900 people. When I found this out—30 minutes before I was to take the stage—my hands began to sweat, my mouth went dry, my knees got weak, chills shot down my back three times, and I could feel my heart beating in my brain. I wanted to hide.

Perhaps appropriately, those 30 minutes were a very active time for my personal prayer life. By God's grace, I made my way to the stage, gave my little testimony, and navigated successfully back to my seat. But here's the astonishing, shameful thing: before I even had a chance to sit back down, I was already trying to decide if I had come off as cool enough, whether the impression I left was going to enhance my reputation or not!

The fear of man is absolute bondage. It dictates our values and the yearnings of our hearts. Because of it, we exalt the opinions of others and spend ridiculous amounts of energy trying to establish ourselves as pitiful little gods in our own narrow little worlds. It is the precise opposite of the fear of the Lord, because it is nothing less than an outright rejection of his Lordship. I cannot begin to tell you how many impure motives I've had, how many silly things I've done, how many slanderous things I've said, how many inappropriate jokes I've laughed at, and how many moral boundaries I've crossed in my lifetime—all because of this unholy fear.

So the fear of man is clearly a snare, and it comes in two varieties: the snare of the world and the snare of the Pharisee.

The Snare of the World

The world ensnares the Sunday Christian—one who feasts at the table of the world throughout the week but masquerades as a follower of Jesus on Sundays. With affections divided, this person lives for the approval of the world and will go to amazing lengths to gain it. His friendships are chosen according to what makes him feel best or most confident. Choosing the world over God, he or she ignores the warnings in James 4:4, "Do you not know that friendship with the world is enmity with God? Therefore whoever wishes to be a friend of the world makes himself an enemy of God," and in Proverbs 13:20, "Whoever walks with the wise becomes wise, but the companion of fools will suffer harm."

Richard Baxter described the snare of the world this way:

> No man is taken for so great a friend to the proud as their admirers; whatever else they be, they love those men best, that highliest esteem them: the faults of such they can extenuate and easily forgive. Let them be drunkards, or whoremongers, or swearers, or otherwise ungodly, the proud man loveth them according to the measure of their honoring him. If you would have his favour, let him hear that you have magnified him behind his back, and that you honour him above all over men.[28]

The Snare of the Pharisee

John 12 tells us about a group of Christians who fell right into the snare of the Pharisee. Some saw Jesus' signs and heard his words and had come to believe in him—"{?many even of the authorities believed in him, but for fear of the Pharisees they did not confess it, so that they would not be put out of the synagogue; for they loved the glory that comes from man more than the glory that comes from God" (John 12:42-43).

These men drew criticism from John because they longed for the approval of men more than the approval of God. They did not fear God—they feared the disapproval of men, specifically the disapproval of the Pharisees. Isn't this backwards? Jesus often criticized the Pharisees for obsessing over outward appearance at the expense of cleaning what really mattered—the stuff inside. Yet when the pressure was on, believing authorities chose the approval of these Pharisees over the approval of the real God. While Paul spoke of presenting ourselves as "holy and acceptable to God," these men were only concerned with what's "holy and acceptable" to the Pharisees.

This is backwards thinking. Yet this type of hypocrisy can easily sneak into a church, setting up snares all around the fellowship hall. This person wants the pastor to notice him. He flaunts his holiness, his theology, his ministry resume, and his supposed humility, all to be deemed holy and acceptable to the pastor, the elders, the congregation— you name it. Why isn't God on that list?

The Struggle for Glory

To choose the snare of the world or the snare of the Pharisee is to choose the glory of creatures over the glory that comes from the Creator. This may not surprise us, for man is deeply and thoroughly fallen, yet it should never-theless shock and appall us, just as it does the heavens:

> Be appalled, O heavens, at this;
>   be shocked, be utterly desolate, declares the LORD,
> for my people have committed two evils:
> they have forsaken me,
>   the fountain of living waters,
> and hewed out cisterns for themselves,
>   broken cisterns that can hold no water.
> (Jeremiah 2:12-13)

To choose a leaky bowl over the eternal fountain of

living waters is to make the heavens gape in horror. But this is what we do when we choose the snare of the fear of man over the freedom to be found in the Lord.

Like the folks in John 12, we want the glory that comes from men. We want it so much that if the only way to gain man's approval is to act in such a way that merits God's disapproval, then that is what we will do. We prefer the favor of man over the favor of God.

Why do we struggle with this so badly? Why do we choose the leaky cisterns? Why do even the most godly among us crave the praise of men? Is it merely the praise we want? Or could it be more?

The Bible tells us that we were made for glory. And that's what we're after. We want glory, we want significance, we want approval. We thirst for it. It's the natural desire of the human heart.

Consider that Adam and Eve had this in the garden. Psalm 8 tells us that God has crowned humanity with glory and honor. In the Garden, before the fall, Adam and Eve experienced all aspects of humanity in perfection. There, fully at peace with God and untouched by sin, they knew complete glory and complete honor. But when tempted by sin they came to believe that even that perfection was insufficient. They chose to sin and subvert the created order, and they lost that complete glory and honor.

We have all continually craved what we lost ever since we lost it. Marked by our sin inherited from Adam, we have trouble believing that the glory and honor that God provides are sufficient and better than the glory and honor we think we can receive from men. Offered perfect acceptance from God through the cross of his Son, we continually repeat the tragic error of Adam and Eve by choosing to run after some other glory, some other honor, rather than abide in what we already have in God.

This is why we hit the malls, practice our lines, flaunt our achievements, and update our Facebook profiles. We scrape the bottom of the cistern for anything that will improve our image, our reputation, or our self-esteem. But at the core of this impulse is the fear of man, and it is a wicked snare that the heavens find appalling.

Who Is Your Lord?

This rummaging for glory is, practically speaking, another way of searching for a savior. That's exactly what the fear of man is. Welch writes that we don't normally think of other people as idols as such, but in fact, "people are our favorite idol. We exalt them and their perceived power above God. We worship them as ones who have God-like exposing gazes … or God-like ability to "fill" us with esteem, love, admiration, acceptance, respect, and other psychological desires." [29]

These idols are cracked cisterns — never reliable — and they leave us empty, craving for more. This is why Calvin cleverly referred to the human heart as a "perpetual factory of idols." [30]

Idols never satisfy. Yet we turn to people as idols, as if somehow they possess the power to fix us. Tragically, the only power held by this idol is the power to ensnare us. Remember the second part of Proverbs 29:25 — "The fear of man lays a snare, but *whoever trusts in the LORD is safe.*" How do we become safe? Not in creatures but in our Creator. For the Christian, he is an eternal refuge and strength, and the only true Deliverer.

As we saw earlier from Luke 12, Jesus warned his disciples, "I tell you, my friends, do not fear those who kill the body, and after that have nothing more that they can do. But I will warn you whom to fear: fear him who, after he has killed, has authority to cast into hell. Yes, I tell you, fear him!" (Luke 12:4-5)

Your first concern should be God's opinion of your thoughts, words, motives, and deeds. What man thinks is not unimportant, but it is absolutely and always secondary to what God thinks. Much of the time, we go through life with those priorities reversed. Our position before men, and our opinion and our reputation in the eyes of men, is never properly our first concern.

Perhaps we do not really understand what God has done for us in order to right our priorities. Paul's words in Romans 8:32 are striking here, particularly as the first part of the verse collides with the second part: "He who did not spare his own Son but gave him up for us all, how will he not also with him graciously give us all things?" As Jesus hung on the cross, God did not merely withhold mercy, he inflicted upon his Son the severest possible punishment, holding back nothing. Jesus was a divine offering of sin for the ungodly enemies of a holy God. God poured out on him the full measure of the wrath that we deserved. Divine justice and divine mercy met in this cosmic display of scandalous grace that has echoed throughout the ages.

But in the second part of that verse, we see that the God who orchestrated such authoritative, appropriate, vengeful cosmic justice then turns around to give you and me "all things." Now that's astonishing!

What is there to fear in life above a holy God who forgives the sins of his wretched enemies? Is the fear of this holy God not better than the fear of that friend who would approve of your sinful words and actions? Is it not better than the approval of that special group that spends so much time concerned with fashion and popularity and the things of this world? Do you really need to be loved for your ability to flatter and impress? Do you really need that coworker's attention? Do you really need your neighbor's envy? Do you need to covet his things? Has God not graciously given us all things? Yes, he has. He most graciously has given us everything needed for life and godliness (2 Peter 1:3).

Christian, the infinite God of the heavens is *for* you. Who else can be against you? Who else do you *need*?

Eight

THE GOD WHO CALMS THE STORMS

There I was, sitting in my cubicle, click-clacking away at my keyboard, following up with clients and counting down the minutes until I entered lunch break freedom. Then I felt it. The ground underneath me began to shake. My coffee started to ripple. The ceiling panels rattled. In ten seconds it was over. Just a little earthquake action, no big deal. Happens a lot in California. Back to work.

Twenty minutes later, the co-worker I shared a cubicle wall with came running into the office. "Did you feel that?!" she yelled to everyone.

"Yup. Earthquake," we replied.

"That was sooooo cool! Like ... the ground moved!"

I had forgotten she wasn't from these parts. Although it had been a mild earthquake, it was special for this Midwestern girl—amazing, even. She couldn't get over it.

I'm not amazed by earthquakes anymore, although maybe I should be. But my co-worker was right. The ground did actually move, and the scooting of massive tectonic plates really is pretty amazing.

Earthquake Passages

Some two thousand years prior, there had been another seeming rupture in the fabric of nature. A savage storm broke out on the Sea of Galilee and nearly swallowed a tiny boat of disciples, along with Jesus of Nazareth. Then, more quickly than it even started, it was over, miraculously calm. Have you read that story? Lots of times? Maybe it has become for you like just another earthquake to a jaded Californian.

But there is a wealth of practical theology in this passage, the point of the story centering on the power and authority of Jesus. What does Jesus say? What does he do? What did it mean for his disciples? What does it mean today? Who is this fearsome Savior? These are pressing questions that should grab our attention and shake us up like a Magnitude 8.

Not long before the boat incident, Jesus had kicked off his public ministry by healing and preaching throughout the region, and word of him had begun to spread rapidly. The disciples followed him every step of the way and as Jesus' ministry grew, as he performed miracle after miracle, no doubt their faith grew, too. After all, they had observed Jesus' authority over disease in the healings of many—the leper, the paralytic, the man with the crippled hand, the Centurion, Peter's mother-in-law, and several others (Mark 1:34). They had also witnessed the unique power with which Jesus preached. At the close of his

Sermon on the Mount, we read that "the crowds were astonished at his teaching, for he was teaching them as one who had authority, and not as their scribes" (Matthew 7:28-29). From the authority of his words to his awesome works, Jesus was unlike anybody the disciples—or anyone else—had ever seen.

In Mark 4, we read of the disciples' particular amazement, one characterized by holy fear:

> On that day, when evening had come, he said to them, "Let us go across to the other side." And leaving the crowd, they took him with them in the boat, just as he was. And other boats were with him. And a great windstorm arose, and the waves were breaking into the boat, so that the boat was already filling. But he was in the stern, asleep on the cushion. And they woke him and said to him, "Teacher, do you not care that we are perishing?" And he awoke and rebuked the wind and said to the sea, "Peace! Be still!" And the wind ceased, and there was a great calm. He said to them, "Why are you so afraid? Have you still no faith?" And they were filled with great fear and said to one another "Who then is this, that even the wind and the sea obey him?" (Mark 4:35-41)

This wasn't the first time Jesus had exerted his will over water. At the wedding of Cana, he had turned water into wine—amazing enough, but nothing like this. This was the definition of epic, the epitome of awesome.

Middle of a Storm

Why were the disciples filled with such fear? Did they not have any faith? When the storm waters rose and started to rock the boat, Jesus the God-man was napping. Terrified, the disciples turned to Jesus and woke him: "Teacher, do you not care that we are perishing?" Of course, he did. And with the sheer rebuke of his word, "Peace! Be still," the wind ceased, the storm subsided, and he saved them.

Have you ever felt like the disciples did in that boat? You've left the carnal pleasures of life to be with Jesus. You're following him with every ounce of energy you can muster, and then, suddenly, a storm sweeps in. In what seems like moments, everything goes from calm and peaceful to crazy. Pain, struggling, stress, confusion, fear — out of nowhere.

You feel as though you may drown as the waves leap all around you, and you think, "Lord, do you not care that I am perishing?" Or perhaps your response is less melodramatic: "Lord, why is this happening to me?" What do we do in moments like this? In days or months or years like this? What the disciples did is always a good place to start. Turn to Jesus.

I imagine the disciples thought they had good reason to be afraid. Even the psalmists and prophets of old found themselves in situations where they felt hopeless. David lamented: "My tears have been my food day and night, while they say to me continually, 'Where is your God?'" (Psalm 42:3). Another psalmist asked, "Why are you cast down, O my soul, and why are you in turmoil within me?" (Psalm 43:5). Isaiah tried to "wake up" the LORD just as the disciples did in the boat: "Awake, awake, put on strength, O arm of the LORD; awake, as in days of old, the generations of long ago" (Isaiah 51:9). Where is God in these moments of despair?

If your life experience has been anything like mine, you've asked this same question. Where is Jesus when the waves rise in our lives? The answer is same as it was for the disciples. He's right there with you in the middle of the storm.

Indeed, God *allows* storms to come. He allows suffering. He allows tragedy. He allows death. This is important. Some teach that if you just muster enough faith you can evade tragedy, sickness, and suffering. I know a young man who fell prey to this wicked teaching. Convinced he "didn't have enough faith" for God to rid him of his depression, he tried to take his own life. While I am thankful to say that he failed, such foul teachings on suffering in the context of this fallen world are tragic for all concerned, and they are an insult to the glory of God. A biblical understanding of suffering is important in our pursuit of godly fear.

Closing his Sermon on the Mount, Jesus tells the story of two very different men who endure suffering:

> Everyone then who hears these words of mine and does them will be like a wise man who built his house on the rock. And the rain fell, and the floods came, and the winds blew and beat on that house, but it did not fall, because it had been founded on the rock. And everyone who hears these words of mine and does not

do them will be like a foolish man who built his house on the sand. And the rain fell, and the floods came, and the winds blew and beat against that house, and it fell, and great was the fall of it. (Matthew 7:24-27)

Which man escaped the storm? Neither. For both men, the rain fell, the floods came, and the winds beat down. Pretty clear message, isn't it? As Christians, we will inevitably suffer such stuff. Storms and earthquakes aren't just for the unbeliever or the unusually wicked. Many of them are simply products of a fallen and cursed world, so get ready—they *will* come. The difference for the Christian is this: we have heard the words of Jesus and built our lives upon his firm foundation. We are safe from ultimate destruction because we are founded on the Rock.

Who Is This Christ?

The abrupt ending to the storm in Mark 4 put the disciples over the top. In addition to the teachings and the healings, Jesus was now exercising direct, immediate control over the weather. His response to their astonishment was much like words Yahweh had spoken to Job thousands of years earlier:

Who shut in the sea with doors
when it burst out from the womb,
when I made clouds its garment
and thick darkness its swaddling band,
and prescribed limits for it
and set bars and doors,

and said, "Thus far shall you come, and no farther,
and here shall your proud waves be stayed"?
(Job 38:8-11)

As with Yahweh to Job, so with Christ to his shocked
disciples. The infinite speaks to the finite, as if to say, "Have
you not believed in me and seen my power? Have you not
experienced my majesty, seen my wisdom, and beheld my
glory?" Job had seen the glory of the sea and still doubted
God's power. The disciples had seen Jesus perform miracle
after miracle, and they had heard him preach with authority,
yet they were still uncertain about his power and goodness.

But once Jesus calmed the winds and settled the sea,
his disciples sat there in amazement, having beheld the
fulfillment of Psalm 107:

Some went down to the sea in ships,
    doing business on the great waters;
they saw the deeds of the LORD,
    his wondrous works in the deep.
For he commanded and raised the stormy wind,
    which lifted up the waves of the sea.
They mounted up to heaven; they went down to the
depths;
    their courage melted away in their evil plight;
they reeled and staggered like drunken men
    and were at their wits' end.
Then they cried to the LORD in their trouble,
    and he delivered them from their distress.
He made the storm be still,

> and the waves of the sea were hushed.
> Then they were glad that the waters were quiet,
> and he brought them to their desired haven.
> (Psalm 107:23-30)

As Jews, the disciples knew their psalms, so they quickly arrived at the realization that the power of Yahweh was in the boat with them. One moment, Jesus is asleep in the vessel; the next moment, he is wielding the power of the great I AM against the seas. Disoriented, they were filled with reverential fear. No wonder they asked, "Who then is this?"

Sovereign over Storms

If God is sovereign over the storms, why does he allow them in the first place? Why not use his limitless power to keep them at bay?

Storms come into the Christian's life for many sanctifying reasons. They can form us into the character, image, and likeness of Christ (Romans 5:3-5). They can shape us to share in suffering and comfort (2 Corinthians 1:7). Most importantly though, God allows the storms to come so that we will relinquish all self-hope and trust in him alone.

When Paul and his friends were blindsided by the storms of life, he echoed this encouragement to the Corinthian church:

> For we do not want you to be ignorant, brothers, of the affliction we experienced in Asia. For we were so utterly burdened beyond our strength that we

despaired of life itself. Indeed, we felt that we had received the sentence of death. But that was to make us rely not on ourselves but on God who raises the dead. He delivered us from such a deadly peril, and he will deliver us. On him we have set our hope that he will deliver us again. (2 Corinthians 1:8-10)

The believer who is awakened to the mighty hand of God has no good reason to be afraid in any storm. Even so, we know how easy it is to lose sight of our hope in Jesus, the Rock of Ages. We are prone to doubt, especially in the middle of a storm. If this is you, cling to Jesus, who calms the storms. If he seems "asleep," wait upon him and trust him. He said that all things will work for your good (Romans 8:28). Claim that. Echo the plea of the father of the boy with the unclean spirit: "I believe; help my unbelief!" (Mark 9:24)

The narrative in Mark 4 ends with the main point. The purpose of the storm was to demonstrate who this man was. "Who then is this, that even the wind and the sea obey him?"

Who is this Jesus?

- He is the manifestation of the glory of God (John 2:11).
- He is the one who upholds the universe (Hebrews 1:3).
- He is the one who holds all things together (Colossians 1:7).
- He is the one who possesses all authority (Matthew 28:18).
- He is our great God and Savior (Titus 2:13).

Jesus is Lord over the storms and over what you fear more than anything else. The disciples began with a fear misplaced, looking at the storms of life. Shortly thereafter, they trembled before the power of the Messiah. Unholy fear was replaced with holy, Christ-exalting fear. Their perspective was corrected. Jesus is in charge. God alone is the one who is sovereign over all.

What is your greatest fear? What looms before you as your greatest potential suffering? Your greatest dread? Your greatest storm? Your only hope from it all is the one who has the power to command, "Peace! Be still!"

Do you want this Jesus in your boat? Who wouldn't? He is the one who calms the storm.

Horatio Spafford lived this truth in a way that few other men have. (If you've heard his story, it is well worth revisiting.) Spafford was a godly man whom God saw fit to draw through horrific suffering. In a short time, he lost nearly everything. His thriving business was destroyed in the Great Chicago Fire. Shortly afterward, his three daughters drowned in the Atlantic Ocean when their ship, en route to England, collided with another ship. His wife barely escaped with her life.

When Spafford learned the devastating news, he immediately departed for England to join his wife in mourning. During the voyage, the ship's captain alerted him as their vessel passed over the site of the collision. Gazing upon the sea that had claimed his daughters' lives, Spafford's eyes filled with tears. Overwhelmed with sorrow, he retreated to the ship's cabin. There in a small, dark corner, broken under the weight of grief, Spafford's heart surrendered to his only sure refuge as he penned the famous words:

> When peace, like a river, attendeth my way,
> When sorrows like sea billows roll;
> Whatever my lot, Thou has taught me to say,
> It is well, it is well, with my soul. [31]

Could you say the same? Join the disciples in Mark 4 as they marvel at the one who *can* calm every storm.

Nine

THE GOD-FEARING CHURCH

I'm sure he had no idea his comment would make such an impression on me. We were in the middle of the tiny, beautiful country of Rwanda. I was leading a small team on a mission trip for a few weeks, and this particular day we were en route to meet the mayor of an influential town in the area. The town had needs, and the churches that sponsored our trip wanted to serve this community for the sake of the gospel. Our team was hoping to help forge that partnership. I was reviewing the day's agenda with our translator when I asked him to tell me what he knew about the mayor we were to meet.

With excitement in his eyes, he replied in his thick African accent, "Oh, you will enjoy this gentleman. He is a great man. A God-fearing man."

A God-fearing man. That was the first time I had ever heard the phrase used aloud. It was endearing. Galvanizing, even. I thought to myself, "I want to be a God-fearing man."

What Happened to the God-Fearers?

I don't think this phrase, "God-fearing man," is used too much anymore in Christian circles. Not in the West, anyway. I suppose it's kind of old-school. But there was a day when to call someone "God-fearing" was a compliment, a way of indicating that someone took all things pertaining to the Lord seriously and held the Almighty in a place of esteem, of reverence, of awe. Where have the God-fearers gone?

I think our churches could use a revival of sorts in this area. If you talk with those outside the tribes of Christianity, you'll discover that today's Church is not known to be especially God-fearing. With a few exceptions, scrolling through Amazon.com's top Christian books list might paint an even bleaker picture. Judging from the titles, the focus of these top-selling books seems to be far more on the glory of man than it is on the glory of God. Why is that? How did the church that bears Christ's name get to such a sad place?

The book of Acts is full of church families that feared the Lord. At Pentecost, "they devoted themselves to the apostles' teaching and the fellowship, to the breaking of bread and the prayers. And awe came upon every soul" (Acts 2:42-43). Later, we see that "the church throughout all Judea and Galilee and Samaria had peace and was being built up. And walking in the fear of the Lord and in the comfort of the Holy Spirit, it multiplied" (Acts 9:31). Evidently, the church that worships the God of the Bible should be marked by godly fear and reverential worship.

In the mid-twentieth century, A. W. Tozer made an

observation about the church of his day. He lamented that the Church suffered from spiritual numbness:

> [This is] a condition which has existed in the Church for some years and is steadily growing worse. I refer to the loss of the concept of majesty from the popular religious mind. The Church has surrendered her once lofty concept of God and has substituted for it one so low, so ignoble, as to be utterly unworthy of thinking, worshiping men. [32]

Sad to say, I think we can still echo the same sentiments.

A God-Fearing Generation

Today's thriving resurgence in gospel-centered and God-exalting theology is encouraging. With new technologies and a rising army of young church planters, the grace-laden potential for revival could be promising. But what will we make of these new opportunities? Will man-exalting books still crowd the shelves? Or will that change? What will today's generation be known for in 25 or 30 years? Revolutionary and impressive church methods or upholding the timeless gospel? Will we be known for the fear of the Lord, the glory of God's grace in the person of Jesus Christ, or will what was said of the tribe of Judah be true of the evangelical church today: "Do you not fear me? declares the LORD. Do you not tremble before me? … But this people has a stubborn and rebellious heart; they have turned aside and gone away. They do not say in their hearts, 'Let us fear the LORD our God'" (Jeremiah 5:22-24)?

I pray this won't be true of us. Instead, let us each echo the psalmist: "Teach me your way, O LORD, that I may walk in your truth; unite my heart to fear your name" (Psalm 86:11). Is God sovereignly at work among us? Absolutely. But the Bible tells us, and history has shown, that God works in his church through the authority of his Word and the power of his Spirit—the Word that speaks of a God-fearing church and the Spirit that makes her shine like a city on a hill.

Christians, we have a mighty and awesome God:

- He is the God who spoke all creation into existence with the sheer power of his voice.
- He is the preeminent one who can measure the galaxies in the span of his hand and who holds them together with a single thought.
- He is the final and only standard for all that is righteous, holy, and good. He is not measured by the standard: he is the standard.
- He is the holy God of justice who cursed the serpent, the man, and the woman with curses that continue to this day. He is the God who floods planets, burns cities, and parts seas in order to accomplish his divine and perfect purposes.
- He is the God for whom angels cover their faces, prophets bow in worship, apostles faint as dead, and kings cast their crowns.
- He is the all-wise God who crafted his divine plan of redemption that would make fools out of the wise and sages out of the foolish.

- He is the God who left his throne to be despised and rejected by his own creatures, to be tortured at their hands.
- He is the God who did not spare his own Son but gave him up for us all so that he might scandalously adopt his enemies as sons.
- He is the God who can throw men into an eternal lake of fire or choose them for everlasting joy.
- He is the God of whom all creation worships. Of whom the heavens cry, "holy, holy, holy."
- He is the Lord, Yahweh, the Great I am, the covenant God, the transcendent one, the immanent one, the omniscient one, the omnipresent one, the God who is there, the miracle worker, the law giver, the powerful one, the self-contained one, the self-existent one, the divine three-in-one.
- He is the Lord God almighty, and like him there is no other.

Church, do we revere him? Do we worship him? Do our lives, our words, and our works declare to the watching world that this is the God we serve? We are to be the light of the world and a city on a hill, letting our light shine before others so that they may see and glorify our heavenly Father (Matthew 5:16). Do our works tell of this glorious God?

Imagine if our churches lived out our mission in the reality of the fear of the LORD. Imagine that the way in which we worship, fellowship, disciple, serve, and send was in a spirit of godly and reverential fear. What would the church of Jesus look like? After all, he is the King of kings, the Lord of lords, the Prince of Peace, the beginning and the end. And he was the one who told Peter, "on this rock I will build my church, and the gates of hell shall not prevail against it" (Matthew 16:18). Not even death can hold back the elect from getting saved.

The God-Fearing Church Today

Do our churches reflect this? If we walked in this fear of the Lord, would our churches look the same as they do today? Indeed, if we walk in godly fear, our churches should reflect it.

Fear of the Lord will be reflected in the way our churches worship. When our churches fear God, and the watching world sees our worship and hears the songs we sing, then we can expect that "many will see and fear, and put their trust in the LORD" (Psalm 40:3).

Fear of the Lord will be reflected in the way our churches preach the Word of God. Those of us who teach the Word of God are accountable to one of the most sobering passages in all of Scripture: "I charge you in the presence of God and of Christ Jesus, who is to judge the living and the dead, and by his appearing and his kingdom: preach the word" (2 Timothy 4:1-2). In the presence of Jesus, the stakes are life and death. The words we preach ought to be the Word that is written, not our own thoughts driven by the fear of man. Handling the Word that was breathed out by God to shape the life and doctrine of his people is no small task. We handle his Word watchfully, reverentially, but with authority, and we do so by the enabling of the mighty counselor.

Fear of the Lord will be reflected in the way our churches hear the Word of God. After telling the parable of the sower, Jesus says, "Take care then how you hear," for to one listener, "more will be given," and to the other listener, "even what he thinks that he has will be taken away" (Luke 8:18). Just as it is with the preacher, the stakes are high for the listener: they are life and death. The Word of God must be more precious to us than silver or gold.

Fear of the Lord will be reflected in our witness. Jeremiah gave God's people this message from the Lord: "seek the welfare of the city where I have sent you into exile, and pray to the Lord on its behalf, for in its welfare you will find your welfare" (Jeremiah 29:7). In a similar manner, as we have considered earlier, Jesus told his disciples to shine:

> You are the light of the world. A city set on a hill cannot be hidden. Nor do people light a lamp and put it under a basket, but on a stand, and it gives light to all in the house. In the same way, let your light shine before others, so that they may see your good works and give glory to your Father who is in heaven. (Matthew 5:14-16)

Are our churches known for this kind of love and light? Are we too busy tidying up our theology that we don't actually live it? Do we glorify God in our neighborhoods?

Are we known for undefiled religion? That of the James 1:27 sort: "Religion that is pure and undefiled before God, the Father, is this: to visit orphans and widows in their affliction, and to keep oneself unstained from the world." There are two parts to that, and we need both. Some of us who emphasize the first part of that command like to flaunt our social works, yet neglect the practice of holiness. Others of us emphasize the second part of that command and end up keeping ourselves unstained in the way a whitewashed tomb is unstained. Jesus lived out both aspects perfectly, and he was quick to call out those who lived a false balance between the two. The God-fearing church will be a faithful witness in both respects: we will engage actively with those in need, but we will not allow the influence of the world to stain us.

Fear of the Lord will be reflected in our ordinances. Consider again Acts 9:31: "So the church throughout all Judea and Galilee and Samaria had peace and was being built up. And walking in the fear of the Lord and in the comfort of the Holy Spirit, it multiplied." The Greek word used for *walking* is *poreu*, which means "to pursue the journey on which one has entered." In imitation of the biblical example of the early church, we are to "pursue the journey" together in ways that are characterized by godly fear. This is a matter of *how* we do things: in our meeting, in our singing, in our baptizing, and in our taking of communion, we ought to have godly fear. We should pursue with reverence all the activities that God has ordained for the church to engage in.

Fear of the Lord will be reflected in our unity. On the night he would be betrayed, Jesus offered this high priestly prayer: "The glory that you have given me I have given to them, that they may be one even as we are one, I in them and you in me, that they may become perfectly one, so that the world may know that you sent me and loved them even as you loved me" (John 17:22-23).

There should be a profound unity among God's people. Is this evident in our local churches? Are we truly "members one of another" (Romans 12:5)? Are we really a body — component parts that need one another? Are we really a family — members who love one another? Do we speak no corrupting talk, but only what builds up, like forgiveness (Ephesians 4:25-32)? Do we "bear one another's burdens" (Galatians 6:2)? Do we keep ourselves from envy, slander, and gossip? Or to use the words of John, will all people know that we are Christians by our love (John 13:35)?

Fear of the Lord will be reflected in our sending. Jesus charged his followers with this commission:

> All authority in heaven and on earth has been given to me. Go therefore and make disciples of all nations, baptizing them in the name of the Father and of the Son and of the Holy Spirit, teaching them to observe all that I have commanded you. And behold, I am with you always, to the end of the age. (Matthew 28:18-20)

Who has the authority of the heavens and earth? Jesus. What does he do? He shares it with us. He commissions his church. And this commissioning King of kings will remain with us on this mission until the end of the age.

Is this the Church we see today? Is this *your* church? This is in no way meant to be a comprehensive account of the church's entire mission in the world, but we did hit the tip of the iceberg. Even so, the point is this: the church is one massive body of blood-bought sinners that have been radically regenerated by the Holy Spirit of the Almighty and have joined in his ministry to go into the world—to every nation, tribe, and tongue—and gather the elect of God until Jesus returns. We are Spirit-filled ambassadors of the gospel. We are his fearsome Church, because he is a fearsome God.

The fear of the Lord is not something that we graduate from—it is something we live in. This holy fear propels us to make much of a holy God, and it empowers us to his holy mission. God-exalting fear is fear that flows from the joys and wonders of the gospel of grace. The fear of the Lord is the beginning of wisdom. The more we fear him, the more we love him. It reminds us who is our Maker, our Sustainer, our Redeemer, our King. And when we look upon his face, we will tremble under the massive weight of his mercy and grace.

> *Holy, holy, holy, is the Lord God Almighty,*
> *who was and is and is to come!*

And this will be our eternal joy. Soli deo gloria.

Endnotes

1. John Bunyan, *The Fear of God* (1679; repr., London:The ReligiousTract Society, 1839), 29.
2. Ibid.
3. John Calvin, *Commentary on the Book of Psalms, vol. 1*, trans. Rev. James Anderson (Edinburgh:The CalvinTranslation Society, 1845), 380.
4. John Calvin, *Institutes of the Christian Religion*, (Grand Rapids, MI: Eerdmans, reprint 1998), 37.
5. E.g., Richard Dawkins, *The God Delusion* (Boston, MA: Houghton Mifflin Harcourt, 2008), 135.
6. A.W.Tozer, *The Knowledge of the Holy* (NewYork: HarperCollins, 1961), 39.
7. Herman Bavinck, *The Doctrine of God*, trans.William Hendriksen (1951; repr., Edinburgh: Banner ofTruth, 1977), 49.
8. C.S. Lewis, *Letters to Malcolm: Chiefly on Prayer* (San Diego: Harvest, 1973), 75.
9. R. C. Sproul, *The Holiness of God* (Carol Stream, IL:Tyndale, 1998), 25-26.
10. Stephen Charnock, *The Existence and Attributes of God* (1853; repr., Grand Rapids: Baker, 2000), 2: 111.
11. Stephen Charnock, *The Existence and Attributes of God* (1853; repr., Grand Rapids: Baker, 2000), 2: 113-114.
12. Ayn Rand, *The Fountainhead* (NewYork: Signet, 1993). 678-679.
13. The Hebrew word *shuwph* in Genesis 3:15 means "to bruise, crush, gape upon."The word is translated as "crush" in the NIV and "bruise" in the ESV, NASB, KJV, and others.
14. G. K. Beale, *The Book of Revelation: A Commentary on the GreekText*, New International GreekTestament Commentary (Grand Rapids, MI: Eerdmans, 1999), 776.
15. D. A. Carson, *Christ and Culture Revisited* (Grand Rapids, MI: Eerdmans, 2008), 46.
16. FromThrice's album *Alchemy Index, Volume II: Water*, (Vagrant, 2008).
17. Some form of the Greek word *hilasterion*, which means "relating to an appeasing, a propitiation, having a placating or expiating force," appears in Romans 3:23-26; Hebrews 2:17; 1 John 2:2; and 1 John 4:10.

18. John 10:15-17; 15:13; 1 John 3:16

19. Keith Getty and StuartTownend, "In Christ Alone," from the album *In Christ Alone* (Kingsway, 2001).

20. Referenced in Charles H. Spurgeon's *The Treasury of David* (New York and London: Funk and Wagnalls, 1885), 77.

21. John Bunyan, "A Treatise on the Fear of God," *The Entire Works of John Bunyan*, ed. Henry Stebbing, vol. 2 (London: James S. Virtue, 1860), 421.

22. Charles Bridges, *An Exposition of the Book of Proverbs*, vol 1, 3rd ed. (London: Beeleys, 1849), 324.

23. D. A. Carson, *Basics for Believers: An Exposition of Philippians* (Grand Rapids, MI: Baker, 1996), 62. Emphasis original to Carson.

24. Edward Mote, first verse and refrain of "My Hope is Built," composed in 1834.

25. John Piper, *Seeing and Savoring Jesus Christ* (Wheaton, IL: Crossway, 2001), 15.

26. Thomas Manton,. *The Complete Works of Thomas Manton*, vol. xi (London: James Nisbet, 1872), 463.

27. Ed Welch, *When People Are Big and God Is Small* (Phillipsburg, NJ: P&R Publishing, 1997), 14.

28. Richard Baxter, *The Practical Works of Richard Baxter, vol. 1* (London: George Virtue, 1838), 203.

29. Ed Welch, *When People Are Big and God Is Small* (Phillipsburg, NJ: P&R Publishing, 1997), 44-45.

30. John Calvin, XI.8, *Institutes of the Christian Religion, vol. 1*, ed. John T. Macneill (Louisville, KY: Westminster John Knox Press, 2006), 108.

31. This story can be found in Robert J. Morgan, *Then Sings My Soul: 150 of the World's Greatest Hymn Stories* (Nashville, TN: Thomas Nelson, 2003), 184-185.

32. A. W. Tozer, *The Knowledge of the Holy* (New York, NY: HarperOne, 1978), vii.

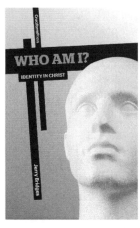

Who Am I?
Identity in Christ

by Jerry Bridges

Jerry Bridges unpacks Scripture to give the Christian eight clear, simple, interlocking answers to one of the most essential questions of life.

"Jerry Bridges' gift for simple but deep spiritual communication is fully displayed in this warm-hearted, biblical spelling out of the Christian's true identity in Christ."

> *J. I. Packer, Theological Editor,* **ESV Study Bible;** *author,* **Knowing God, A Quest for Godliness, Concise Theology**

"I know of no one better prepared than Jerry Bridges to write *Who Am I?* He is a man who knows who he is in Christ and he helps us to see succinctly and clearly who we are to be. Thank you for another gift to the Church of your wisdom and insight in this book."

> *R.C. Sproul, founder, chairman, president, Ligonier Ministries; executive editor,* **Tabletalk** *magazine; general editor,* **The Reformation Study Bible**

"*Who Am I?* answers one of the most pressing questions of our time in clear gospel categories straight from the Bible. This little book is a great resource to ground new believers and remind all of us of what God has made us through faith in Jesus. Thank the Lord for Jerry Bridges, who continues to provide the warm, clear, and biblically balanced teaching that has made him so beloved to this generation of Christians."

> *Richard D. Phillips, Senior Minister, Second Presbyterian Church, Greenville, SC*

Licensed to Kill
A Field Manual for Mortifying Sin

by Brian G. Hedges

**Your soul is a war zone.
Know your enemy.
Learn to fight.**

"A faithful, smart, Word-centered guide."
– *Wes Ward, Revive Our Hearts*

"Are there things you hate that you end up doing anyway? Have you tried to stop sinning in certain areas of your life, only to face defeat over and over again? If you're ready to get serious about sin patterns in your life—ready to put sin to death instead of trying to manage it—this book outlines the only strategy that works. This is a book I will return to and regularly recommend to others."
Bob Lepine, Co-Host, FamilyLife Today

"Brian Hedges shows the importance of fighting the sin that so easily entangles us and robs us of our freedom, by fleeing to the finished work of Christ every day. Well done!"
Tullian Tchividjian, Coral Ridge Presbyterian Church; author, Jesus + Nothing = Everything

"Rather than aiming at simple moral reformation, *Licensed to Kill* aims at our spiritual transformation. Like any good field manual, this one focuses on the most critical information regarding our enemy, and gives practical instruction concerning the stalking and killing of sin. This is a theologically solid and helpfully illustrated book that holds out the gospel confidence of sin's ultimate demise."
Joe Thorn, pastor and author, Note to Self: The Discipline of Preaching to Yourself

Getting Back in the Race
The Cure for Backsliding

by Joel R. Beeke

Backsliding is the worst thing that can happen to anyone claiming faith in Jesus.

Find out why. Learn the diagnosis. Experience the cure.

"This book is a masterpiece, and I do not say that lightly. This excellent work, so helpfully spiced with quotations from the Puritans, needs to be read over and over again. I heartily commend it."
***Martin Holdt, Pastor; editor,* Reformation Africa South**

"Joel Beeke's characteristic clarity, biblical fidelity, and unflinching care as to detail and pastoral wisdom is obvious on every page. This book is an honest and sometimes chilling exposition of the seriousness of backsliding; at the same time, it unfailingly breathes the air of grace and hope. Timely and judicious."
Derek W. H. Thomas, First Presbyterian Church, Columbia, SC; Editorial Director, Alliance of Confessing Evangelicals

"Don't settle for being a spiritual shrimp,' argues Dr. Beeke. The pity is that too many modern Christians are opting for shrimpishly small degrees of grace. Indwelling sin drags the careless believer down into guilty backsliding. This book is a prescription for the believer who feels his guilt."
Maurice Roberts, former editor,* Banner of Truth *magazine

"Dr. Beeke outlines the best means of bringing balm and healing to the backslidden soul. Highly recommended."
Michael Haykin, Professor, Southern Baptist Theo. Sem.

Smooth Stones
Bringing Down the Giant
Questions of Apologetics

by Joe Coffey

Street-level apologetics for everyday Christians.

Because faith in Jesus makes sense. And you don't need an advanced degree to understand why.

"What a thrill for me to see Joe Coffey, a graduate of our first Centurions Program class, apply the biblical worldview principles we teach at BreakPoint and the Colson Center. In this marvelous little book, Joe simply and succinctly lays out the tenets of the Christian faith within the context of the four key life and worldview questions. This is an excellent resource for Christians and non-Christians alike who are seeking the Truth."
> *Chuck Colson, Founder of Prison Fellowship and the Colson Center for Christian Worldview*

"This book may be the best resource I've seen to answer common objections in everyday language."
> *Jared Totten, Critical Thinking Blog*

"A quick read that packs a punch .... I'm always on the lookout for something like this. Smooth Stones is a winner."
> *Mike del Rosario, ApologeticsGuy.Com*

"Most books on apologetics are too long, too deep, and too complicated. This book has none of these defects. Like its title, it is like a smooth stone from David's apologetic sling directed right to the mind of an enquiring reader"
> *Norman L. Geisler, Distinguished Professor of Apologetics, Veritas Evangelical Seminary, Murrieta, CA*

"But God..."
The Two Words at the Heart of the Gospel

by Casey Lute

**Just two words.
Understand their use in Scripture,
and you will never be the same.**

"Rock-solid theology packaged in an engaging and accessible form."
– Louis Tullo, Sight Regained blog

"Keying off of nine occurrences of "But God" in the English Bible, Casey Lute ably opens up Scripture in a manner that is instructive, edifying, encouraging, and convicting. This little book would be useful in family or personal reading, or as a gift to a friend. You will enjoy Casey's style, you will have a fresh view of some critical Scripture, and your appreciation for God's mighty grace will be deepened."
> *Dan Phillips, Pyromaniacs blog, author of The World-Tilting Gospel (forthcoming from Kregel)*

"A refreshingly concise, yet comprehensive biblical theology of grace that left this reader more in awe of the grace of God. "
> *Aaron Armstrong, BloggingTheologically. com*

""Casey Lute reminds us that nothing is impossible with God, that we must always reckon with God, and that God brings life out of death and joy out of sorrow. "
> *Thomas R. Schreiner, Professor of New Testament Interpretation, The Southern Baptist Theological Seminary*

"A mini-theology that will speak to the needs of every reader of this small but powerful book. Read it yourself and you will be blessed. Give it to a friend and you will be a blessing."
> *William Varner, Prof. of Biblical Studies, The Master's College*

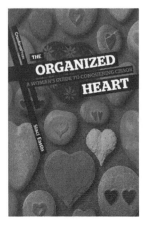

The Organized Heart
A Woman's Guide to Conquering Chaos

by Staci Eastin

**Disorganized?
You don't need more rules, the latest technique, or a new gadget.**

This book will show you a different, better way. A way grounded in the grace of God.

"Staci Eastin packs a gracious punch, full of insights about our disorganized hearts and lives, immediately followed by the balm of gospel-shaped hopes. This book is ideal for accountability partners and small groups."

> *Carolyn McCulley, blogger, filmmaker, author of* Radical Womanhood *and* Did I Kiss Marriage Goodbye?

"Unless we understand the spiritual dimension of productivity, our techniques will ultimately backfire. Find that dimension here. Encouraging and uplifting rather than guilt-driven, this book can help women who want to be more organized but know that adding a new method is not enough."

> *Matt Perman, Director of Strategy at Desiring God, blogger, author of the forthcoming book,* What's Best Next: How the Gospel Transforms the Way You Get Things Done

"Organizing a home can be an insurmountable challenge for a woman. The Organized Heart makes a unique connection between idols of the heart and the ability to run a well-managed home. This is not a how-to. Eastin looks at sin as the root problem of disorganization. She offers a fresh new approach and one I recommend, especially to those of us who have tried all the other self-help models and failed."

> *Aileen Challies, Mom of three, and wife of blogger, author, and pastor Tim Challies*

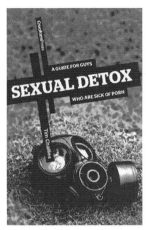

Sexual Detox
A Guide for Guys Who Are Sick of Porn

by Tim Challies

"In an age when sex is worshiped as a god, a little book like this can go a long way to helping men overcome sexual addiction."
–Pastor Mark Driscoll
Mars Hill Church
Acts 29

"Online pornography is not just a problem for Christian men; it is THE problem. Many men, young and old, in our churches need *Sexual Detox*. Challies offers practical, doable and, above all, gospel-centered hope for men. I want every man I serve and all the guys on our staff to read this book."
Tedd Tripp, Pastor, and author of Shepherding a Child's Heart

"Tim Challies strikes just the right balance in this necessary work. His assessment of the sexual epidemic in our culture is sober but not without hope. His advice is practical but avoids a checklist mentality. His discussion of sexual sin is frank without being inappropriate. This book will be a valuable resource."
Kevin DeYoung, Pastor and author

"Thank God for using Tim to articulate simply and unashamedly the truth about sex amidst a culture of permissiveness."
Ben Zobrist, Tampa Bay Rays

"*Sexual Detox* is just what we need. It is clear, honest, and biblical, written with a tone that is knowing but kind, exhortative but gracious, realistic but determined. We have been given by Tim Challies a terrific resource for fighting sin and exalting Christ.
Owen Strachan, Boyce College

Servanthood as Worship
The Privilege of Life in a Local Church

by Nate Palmer

We [serve] because he first [served] us. - 1 John 1:19 [sort of]

What ever happened to servanthood? Here is a biblical presentation of our calling to serve in the church, motivated by the grace that is ours in the gospel.

"In an age where the church can be likened to Cinderella - beautiful, but largely ignored and forgotten - Nate Palmer's brief book forces us to rethink both the church and our relationship to her. In an age where egocentrism ensures we sing, 'O say, can you see - what's in it for me?' on a weekly basis, Palmer forces us to say instead, 'How can I best serve the church?' Looking at the needs of others rather than one's own is possibly the most serious deficiency in the church today. Reading this book will help redress the deficiency. I heartily recommend it."
Derek W.H. Thomas, Professor of Theology, Reformed Theological Seminary (Jackson)

"Think of these pages as a handbook. It contains a sustainable, practical vision for serving in the local church that is powered by grace. Along the way, you'll get a mini theological education."
Justin Buzzard, pastor, San Francisco Bay Area, Buzzard Blog

"In our media-crazed, me-first culture, the art of the basin and the towel has been shoved off onto those who get paid to serve - certainly a call to serve in humility can't be God's will for all of us, or could it? Nate Palmer gets at the heart of our resistance.. I strongly recommend this book."
Elyse Fitzpatrick, author of Because He Loves Me

Made in the USA
San Bernardino, CA
17 January 2013